Nonprofit Boards

NONPROFIT LAW, FINANCE, AND MANAGEMENT SERIES

The Art of Planned Giving: Understanding Donors and the Culture of Giving by Douglas E. White

Charity, Advocacy, and the Law by Bruce R. Hopkins

The Complete Guide to Nonprofit Management by Smith, Bucklin & Associates

Developing Affordable Housing: A Practical Guide for Nonprofit Organizations by Bennett L. Hecht

Financial and Accounting Guide for Not-for-Profit Organizations, Fifth Edition by Malvern J. Gross, Jr., Richard F. Larkin, Roger S. Bruttomesso, John J. McNally, Price Waterhouse LLP

Financial Planning for Nonprofit Organizations by Jody Blazek

Fund-Raising: Evaluating and Managing the Fund Development Process by James M. Greenfield

Fund-Raising Fundamentals: A Guide to Annual Giving for Professionals and Volunteers by James M. Greenfield

Fund-Raising Regulation: A State-by-State Handbook of Registration Forms, Requirements, and Procedures by Seth Perlman and Betsy Hills Bush

Fund-Raising Regulation Report by Bruce R. Hopkins and Betsy Hills Bush

The Law of Fund-Raising, Second Edition by Bruce R. Hopkins

The Law of Tax-Exempt Healthcare Organizations by Thomas K. Hyatt and Bruce R. Hopkins

The Law of Tax-Exempt Organizations, Sixth Edition by Bruce R. Hopkins

The Legal Answer Book for Nonprofit Organizations by Bruce R. Hopkins

A Legal Guide to Starting and Managing a Nonprofit Organization, Second Edition by Bruce R. Hopkins

Managing Affordable Housing: A Practical Guide to Creating Stable Communities by Bennett L. Hecht, Local Initiatives Support Corporation, and James Stockard

Nonprofit Boards: Roles, Responsibilities, and Performance by Diane J. Duca

The Nonprofit Counsel by Bruce R. Hopkins

The Nonprofit Guide to the Internet by Robbin Zeff

The Nonprofit Law Dictionary by Bruce R. Hopkins

Nonprofit Litigation: A Practical Guide with Forms and Checklists by Steve Bachmann

The Nonprofit Management Handbook: Operating Policies and Procedures by Tracy Daniel Connors

The Nonprofit Manager's Resource Dictionary by Ronald A. Landskroner

Nonprofit Organizations' Business Forms: Disk Edition by John Wiley & Sons, Inc.

Partnerships and Joint Ventures Involving Tax-Exempt Organizations by Michael I. Sanders

Planned Giving: Management, Marketing, and Law by Ronald R. Jordan and Katelyn L. Quynn

Reengineering Your Nonprofit Organization: A Guide to Strategic Transformation by Alceste T. Pappas

Reinventing the University: Managing and Financing Institutions of Higher Education by Sandra L. Johnson and Sean C. Rush, Coopers & Lybrand, L.L.P.

Streetsmart Financial Basics for Nonprofit Managers by Thomas A. McLaughlin

Successful Marketing Strategies for Nonprofit Organizations by Barry J. McLeish

The Tax Law of Charitable Giving by Bruce R. Hopkins

Tax Planning and Compliance for Tax-Exempt Organizations: Forms, Checklists, Procedures, Second Edition by Jody Blazek

The Volunteer Management Handbook by Tracy Daniel Connors

Nonprofit Boards: Roles, Responsibilities, and Performance

Diane J. Duca

John Wiley & Sons, Inc.

New York · Chichester · Brisbane · Toronto · Singapore · Weinheim

This text is printed on acid-free paper.

Building Board Diversity and *A Snaphsot of America's Nonprofit Boards* are available from the National Center for Nonprofit Boards, 2000 L Street, NW, Suite 510, Washington, D.C., 20026. Telephone: 202-452-6262

Library of Congress Cataloging in Publication Data:
Duca, Diane J.
    Nonprofit boards : roles, responsibilities, and performance/ Diane J. Duca.
        p. cm.—(Nonprofit law, finance, and management series)
    Includes index.
    ISBN 0-471-13020-6 (cloth)
    1. Nonprofit organizations.   2. Directors of corporations.
3. Corporate governance.   I. Title.   II. Series.
HD2769.15.D83   1996
658.4'22—dc20   96-23264

Printed in the United States of America

10 9 8 7 6 5 4 3 2

Contents

Preface   ix

Prologue   1

Chapter One: Models of Governance and Leadership   3
Tripartite System: A Conventional Model of Governance   4
An Alternative Governance-Theory Model   5
The Cyclical Board Model   7
Leadership or Management   10
   Boards as Leaders or Managers   11
   Assessing Nonprofit Leadership   14
Suggestions for Further Reading   15

**Chapter Two: Accountability: A Board's Fiduciary
Obligations**   17
Accountability Issues   17
   Board and Executive Accountability   18
Legal Issues and Obligations   20
   The Foundations of a Nonprofit's Operation   20
   A Board's Legal Responsibilities and Liabilities   21
   Regulations   23
   Licensing   24
   Trouble Spots and Red Flags   25
Ethical Obligations   28
Suggestions for Further Reading   32

**Chapter Three: Structuring a Board for Maximum
Effectiveness**   35
Board Size   36
   Demographics of Board Size   36
   The Issue of Board Size   37

The Composition of Boards   39
    Building a Diverse Board   41
Supportive Structures   43
    Advisory Bodies   43
    Foundation Boards   46
    Voting Memberships   47
Changing Structure to Meet Changing Needs: A Case
    Study   48
Suggestions for Further Reading   54

Chapter Four: Organizing the Board's Work   55
Working Structures   55
    The Role of Committees   56
    Types of Board Committees   57
    Traditional Board Committees and their Functions   58
    An Alternative Way to Organize Board Work   61
    Rules for Effective Committees   62
Board Development   63
    The Benefits of an Educated Board   63
    Orientation of New Members   64
    Training and Sustaining Board Members   66
Suggestions for Further Reading   67

**Chapter Five: The Core Responsibilities of a Nonprofit
Board   69**
Policies and Plans   69
    The Nature of Policy   69
    Setting Policy   71
    Long-Range and Strategic Planning   73
    A Board's Role in Planning   75
    Strategies for Planning   76
Fiscal Matters and Fund-Raising   80
    Budgeting and the Board   81
    Fiscal Oversight Responsibilities of a Board   82
    A Board's Fund-Raising Role   82
    The Impact of Changes in the Resource
        Environment   84
Suggestions for Further Reading   87

Chapter Six: Building a Cooperative Spirit 89

Perspectives on Board-Executive Relationships 89
Executive Focus on Board Behaviors 91
A Balanced Partnership 92
Strong Boards and Strong Executives 93
Effective Communication 95
Human Resource Management in the Boardroom 95
The Role of the Chairperson 96
Management of Conflict 97
Reciprocity in Practice: A Case Study 98
Suggestions for Further Reading 100

Chapter Seven: Effective Board Meetings 101

The Importance of Meetings 101
Principles of Effective Meetings 102
Setting Focused Agendas 105
Physical and Procedural Factors 107
Making Quality Decisions 111
Barriers to Effective Decision Making 111
Processes for Effective Decision Making 112
Suggestions for Further Reading 114

Chapter Eight: Maintaining Focus on Mission 117

Mission as a Beginning 117
Staying on Track 119
Benefits of Mission-Focus 120
Mission as an End: A Case Study 121
Evaluation and Assessment 123
A Board's Role in Evaluation 123
Approaching Evaluation 125
Assessing the Executive's Performance 127
A Board's Self-Assessment 129
Suggestions for Further Reading 132

Chapter Nine: New Challenges for Nonprofit Boards 135

Government Relations 135
The Impact of Professionalism 138
Changing Role of the Executive 139
Collaboration and Strategic Alliances 140

    The Trend Toward Mergers   143
    Mission Matters When Merging: A Case Study   145
Improving Nonprofits' Image   148
Suggestions for Further Reading   150

Appendixes   153

    Appendix A: Types of Tax-Exempt Organizations Under U.S.
    Law   155
    Appendix B: Immunity from Civil Liability: Section 5, Florida
    Statute 617.0285 (1987)   157
    Appendix C: Code of Organizational Ethics: The Hospice of
    the Florida Suncoast   159
    Appendix D: Letter of Agreement: Agency Access
    Development Project (AADP)   161
    Appendix E: The 9-Box Tool for Assessing Perceptions   167
    Appendix F: Decision Flow: Municipal League   169
    Appendix G: Organizational Cycle: Municipal
    League/Foundation   171
    Appendix H: Idea-Generating Techniques   173
    Appendix I: Position Specification: Northwest Network for
    Youth   175

Notes   181

Index   187

Preface

This book offers the chief executives and boards of directors of nonprofit organizations different perspectives on board structure, composition, roles, functions, and various approaches to fulfilling a board's governance responsibilities. The contemporary issues that challenge a nonprofit organization and its board of directors are discussed, and boards that have made a difference are profiled.

In writing this book, my goals have been to provide readers with different ways for thinking about nonprofit boards and the issues of governance; prompt them to assess their board; and stimulate a desire to reach for higher standards of board performance. Despite statements like "a board must" or "a board needs to," keep in mind that there is no one right way (legal matters excepted) to manage the business of a board, or one superior model of governance. In today's complex and interdependent society, a contingency approach to organizational management and board governance offers more options for resolving problems.

All nonprofit organizations are challenged by two sets of issues. The first is the acquisition of sufficient resources to enable the organization to fulfill its mission. Clearly articulated goals and objectives, a positive public image, strategic planning, and collaborative endeavors contribute to an organization's capacity for attracting resources. Organizations lacking in these areas encounter difficulties in raising funds and volunteers to support their cause.

The second issue is making the best use of an organization's existing resources. Sound administrative practices, professionalism among staff, good internal and external communications, and effective board governance contribute to the overall health and well-being of the nonprofit. Organizations that do not use their resources effectively limit their ability to make a social impact on society.

The issues confronting nonprofit organizations may be universal, but resolutions to their problems are not; the contexts in which organizations operate create different responses. The boards of nonprofit organizations can be either part of the problem or part of the solution with respect to the acquisition of resources or use of existing resources.

Letter from a Board Member in British Columbia

November 1, 1995

I came to the two-year board term with the Family Day Care Society by way of a neighbor and past president of this board who decided I would be "good for the place." She set about working on my moral conscience! As I was a single, thirty-nine-year-old woman who had never had children, I wondered just how qualified I was for this role, but was reassured heartily that my experience as director of a nursing education program was pertinent. Anyway, I signed up.

In general I enjoyed my term of office, gained many insights about "families' and mothers' " struggle for decent day-care services, and discovered some of the inner conflicts and tensions to which agencies with vast missions and marginal resources are constantly exposed.

The service provided by this society was to recruit family (home-based) day care, to place children in these homes, and to provide follow-up support and evaluation, or "quality control," measures. To carry out this work there were two women and a half-time secretary paid with grant money always threatening to dry up. The society serviced a community of one hundred thousand people. The six-member board met twice a month with staff in the evenings after long work-packed days.

The behavior of the volunteer board members reflected very different orientations toward their role and function, which, never being clarified, made for some strange dynamics. I regularly sought clarification about our role in supporting the staff with their overwhelming responsibilities. And I observed the staff constantly accounting to the board, who seemed to overreact to their sense of public duty for the public purse (i.e., grant money which paid the staff salaries).

In my novice opinion, what was desperately needed from us "volunteers" were resources, advocacy in the community, and hands-on HELP for a shoestring operation; instead, we acted like a judiciary body of advisors and critics. What was clearly missing was volunteer leadership and a consciousness that would exact the talents and resources from this volunteer group so we could be more constructive, have a more direct impact on service, and on the staff. I tried to communicate and perform in a service support–oriented way towards the staff and other board members during my term of office. I realized what a huge task and commitment was needed by board members to really be effective—much more than two meetings a month. I felt frustrated, sad, and regretful that my own career on the war-torn front of nursing in no way allowed me to take this on, so I did not renew my office past the second year. My heart ached for this struggling organization, which clearly saw a need, but was far too short of time, commitment, attitude, and skills needed to be effective.

This letter (reprinted with permission) tells of the struggle faced by many nonprofit organizations and expresses the frustration board members can experience when their roles and responsibilities are not clearly defined. This book was written to offer guidance for all types of nonprofit boards and hope for those who feel overwhelmed by the enormity of their tasks.

Considering that nonprofit boards assume such a variety of roles and functions and exhibit a range of behaviors, it is not surprising that studies attempting to characterize high-performing boards have produced inconclusive results. The roles boards play in contributing to the effective operation of nonprofit organizations varies immensely. What works for one organization is contingent upon that organization's unique environment (including the personalities involved), which no other organization can replicate precisely. Some boards are passive observers at best, while others are actively involved in planning, policy setting, stakeholder relations, and fundraising. Many boards are invisible until there is a crisis that motivates them to act and essentially rescue the organization. Additionally, boards may be either entrepreneurial or averse to risk in their approaches to governance.

Nonprofit boards that take their positions as trustees seriously; understand their roles and functions; apply sound governance practices in managing their affairs; and, establish policies that empower their organizations to fulfill their missions are successful strategic leaders. Nonprofit organizations and their constituents profit when boards know how to govern well; but, more importantly, society ultimately benefits, as the quality of service provided by nonprofits is enhanced.

Nonprofit Boards

Prologue

A nongovernmental organization in the small African nation of Malawi provides an example of the universality of issues faced by nonprofits, a culture-specific response to those issues, and the role played by a board in helping an organization achieve its goals.

Chitukuko Cha A'mayi m'Malawi (CCAM), Women in Development in Malawi, was envisioned by a former Malawian president, Dr. H. Kamuzu Banda, and organized in 1985 by a group of successful, civic-minded women. It began with the full support and protection of the government, including some financial assistance for its projects. While CCAM has always been an independent organization, it would have had great difficulty getting started without the government's support. This affiliation allowed access to expertise that the organization's founding board did not have.

The founding board wanted to provide a vehicle for Malawian women to work together, learn from each other, and develop the quality of their personal lives and of life in their villages. CCAM's mission is "to facilitate the integration of women, especially those in rural areas, into the mainstream of economic development." In Malawi, "integration" refers to the simple act of getting together. Malawi is an agrarian society where people in rural areas rarely travel beyond their districts, or even out of their villages. Women are particularly disadvantaged by this lack of mobility. CCAM provides a unique opportunity for members to meet women from other parts of Malawi. It raises funds to pay for transportation, arranges visits to prototype farms that demonstrate crop rotation and techniques of soil enrichment, and sponsors seminars on income-generating activities. These activities are important steps toward empowering the women of Malawi.

However, CCAM did not anticipate the demand for services beyond those in the area of economic development. A holistic approach was necessary as new sets of needs in such areas as education, health and nutrition, and "family spacing" were identified (e.g., disaster relief, medical supplies, village schools, clothing, HIV prevention education, funeral services). The board of CCAM realized that progress in economic development was contingent upon meeting other basic needs. For example, a woman could not face the problem of selling her crafts in distant markets if she or her children were ill or if her family lacked adequate clothing or shelter.

CCAM operates informally; the board of directors and other volunteers do all of the work of the organization. The board functions as mentor and coordinator for twenty-four districts throughout Malawi. The organization is loosely structured like a grassroots membership organization, in that village women are elected to fill leadership positions. Proposals for projects emerge from the districts. A screening committee of the board decides the merit and feasibility of the proposals and selects those to be adopted by CCAM. Resources in Malawi are limited; CCAM must capture the attention and interest of church groups, foundations, and other out-of-country organizations that support projects in developing nations. Every project CCAM elects to undertake is one of significant need, but in soliciting international support, the organization faces global competition from other developing nations with similar, much-needed projects.

Women with no prior organizational experience have joined CCAM, learned new areas of responsibility, and are reported to have an increased sense of self-worth. This empowerment was possible because of the mentor function of the board. In the Malawian culture, individual recognition "is of less value than the value of the whole," which means that board members, including the chairperson (former Official Hostess Mama C. Tamanda Kadzamira) assume a low profile. The organization's many successful projects are attributed to the cooperation among all of its participants.[1]

CHAPTER ONE

Models of Governance and Leadership

B oard service is set in a tradition of volunteerism with ancient Judeo-Christian roots. In this country, service on a volunteer board of directors has become a traditional form of citizen participation in both the public and private sectors; as such, boards contribute to an evolving democratic process. For nonprofit boards in particular, an individual who chooses to serve takes on the role of a trustee of community values. Although a nonprofit board of directors may govern only one organization, it has a public service duty to the entire community. Consider, for example, that the boards of trustees of universities are entrusted with education and boards of directors of hospitals are entrusted with health care. Notwithstanding their power and value, volunteer boards of directors are essentially human institutions and thus subject to criticism. Perhaps because of the criticism leveled at boards, or perhaps in response to the shifting paradigm in human services, more boards are taking a closer look at how they operate.

Nonprofit boards exist because they are basic to corporate organization. But their existence may well be the only characteristic that nonprofit boards of directors have in common; boards are as diverse as the organizations they govern. A board may be a curse or a boon to an organization, depending on how it is used or not used, the level of commitment among board members, how members exercise leadership, or any number of other factors. When there is trouble in the boardroom, it may be either a people-problem or a problem of the governing process.

The term *governing* applied to a board of directors refers to its legal right to exercise authority over some organization. *Governance* is how a board goes about exercising its authority over an organization; it is a system or process for managing a board's affairs. A conventional model and an alternative model of board governance, along with a different way of thinking about board behavior, are presented in this chapter. Before considering specific aspects of governance, such as a board's roles, responsibilities, and performance, it is useful to reflect on the perceptions a board may have of itself. Does a board think of itself strictly as a policy-setting body, or as an active working board? Do board members consider themselves leaders or managers? Does a board exhibit a take-charge kind of behavior, or is it generally more passive? A board's self-image influences its behavior. If a board wants to improve or modify its way of governing, it should begin with an understanding of its perceptions of governance and board behavior.

TRIPARTITE SYSTEM: A CONVENTIONAL MODEL OF GOVERNANCE

Cyril Houle, author of several books and articles on nonprofit boards, offers a contemporary approach to a conventional perspective of board governance. He points out that organizational growth necessitates more pronounced divisions of responsibility. In many nonprofits, the responsibilities for running the organization evolve into a three-part, interactive system—a *tripartite system*—comprised of a board of directors, an executive, and staff. If this system is to function effectively, its parts need to share a sense of mission. A board's central function is to keep the organization's mission in focus, and its primary responsibility is to ensure that the other parts of the system are working toward accomplishing that mission.[1] This is a conventional perspective of a board's central function and primary responsibility. The contemporary aspect of Houle's board model is his focus on facilitative rather than controlling board behaviors.

Some nonprofit boards take their charge of ultimate responsibility for an organization so much to heart that they also attempt to run it. Ultimate authority and responsibility does not mean ultimate control. Houle says that, for a nonprofit board of directors, aiding and supporting an organization is a more appropriate stance than control. Board energies should be directed toward *fostering activities,* those that help an organization advance its mission and goals, including:

- planning for the future
- interpreting the organization's mission to the public

- exercising influence in "the halls of government"
- setting broad policies
- deliberating options for action
- contracting for the executive
- soliciting prospective contributors
- dealing proactively with emerging issues.

In carrying out these activities, "care must be taken neither to lay too heavy a burden on already busy [board] people nor to allow too willing board members to assume more responsibility than they should carry. The role of the trustee is important but it is also part-time." [2]

The tripartite system model promotes a balanced relationship between an executive and a board of directors. There is an old adage that says if you have a strong board you don't need a strong executive and vice versa. Or, if either the board or executive is too powerful, one must be made less powerful in order to regain a balanced relationship. Neither of these supposed truisms makes sense. An effective nonprofit organization has both a strong board of directors and a strong executive, and this strength is mutually valued. Leadership does not rest solely in the board's domain any more than it does in the executive-staff domain; leadership should emanate from both the board and the executive. See Chapter 6 for further discussion of board-staff relationships.

AN ALTERNATIVE GOVERNANCE-THEORY MODEL

John Carver's work in developing models of board governance spans two decades; his policy-focused framework for governance has become known simply as *Carver's model.* The following section outlines Carver's model (also referred to as the governance-theory model), with its underlying premises, and suggests why an organization might consider its application.

The cornerstone of Carver's governance-theory model is a redefinition of policy and a board's policy-making process. A board must be concerned primarily with policy in order to stay close to the center of the organization's meaning or what it values. In Carver's words, "Because policies permeate and dominate all aspects of organizational life, they present the most powerful lever for the exercise of leadership." [3]

What is needed, according to Carver, is not a set of corrective practices to improve the way a board operates, but rather a totally new concept of board work, leadership, and a theory of governance. He argues for "dissatisfaction with what we now accept as ordinary," and says that "the problems [with boards] lie squarely in our widely accepted approach to governance." [4] He outlines a way for boards to transform their work habits and enhance their strategic leadership.

When a board exercises its leadership by setting explicit policies, it governs more effectively for several reasons:

1. A policy focus brings efficiency and leverage to a board of directors. The more time a board spends on resolving specific problems, the less time it has to devote to the larger issues. Focusing on policies as the core element of an organization uses a board's time more effectively. Instead of devoting a block of precious meeting time to discussing the pros and cons of, and options for, expanding hours of operation, discussion should focus on what policy is driving the move toward expanded service.

2. Budgets, long-range plans, and program evaluations brought to the board for deliberation and action are *materials*. A board that addresses the policies underlying these materials, rather than the materials' content, deals directly with organizational fundamentals that are more enduring by nature.

3. Boards need members who are unafraid to ask questions about the value of one alternative over another. They should not become preoccupied with seeking new members whose expertise matches the administrative or functional areas of an organization. This approach to board composition is a wasted effort from the Carver model perspective, because a board governing through policy does not need to focus on that kind of expertise.

According to the governance-theory perspective, policy-making should be guided by questions about governance and not administrative details. An organization's governing body should envision the future; its leaders should feel free to dream. Closely examining a budget line by line is neither visionary nor inspirational. Organizing the details of a special event may be fun, but it does not speak to an organization's future.

There are certain categories into which policies can be grouped, but they should not be thought of as policies about finance, personnel, and so forth. Policies should instead be characterized as:

- ends to be achieved
- means to those ends
- the board-staff relationship
- the process of governance itself.[5]

Such an approach will divert boards from micromanaging their organization, keep them focused on the future, and facilitate dialogue about organizational values. This requires commitment to a new way of thinking about the work of a board of directors. While policy-making may be a central function of nonprofit boards, it is not their only function. A board needs to utilize policy to evaluate the executive's performance, engage in fund-raising, and interact with the organization's external environment.

THE CYCLICAL BOARD MODEL

Boards of directors tend to behave in a certain way depending on their stage of development, as well as the state of the organization. Sometimes they behave like managers and at other times they act more like leaders. Unlike the governance-theory model and the tripartite system model, which offer principles of board governance, the *cyclical board model* describes categories of board behavior. The model, proposed by scholar Miriam Wood, integrates ideas about board-staff relations, board effectiveness, and board members' values.

In Wood's model, a nonrecurring founding period is followed by a sequence of three distinct operating phases punctuated by a series of crises that reinitiates the sequence. "During each cycle, board members become progressively less interested in the agency's mission and programs and more interested in the board's bureaucratic procedures and the agency's reputation for success in the community." [6] Exhibit 1.1 summarizes the characteristics of boards of directors at various stages.

Wood studied twenty-one nonprofit organizations and discovered that their *sequence* of cycles (and the stages within each cycle) was predictable but that their *timing* was not; boards tended to get stuck in one stage or another. Only three of the nonprofits sampled had gone through a repetition of cycles, and these were organizations with a long history of operation—82, 124, and 136 years. It is inappropriate to make generalizations to a universe of nonprofit boards from a sample of twenty-one. Nonetheless, Wood's empirical-based findings support what others have intuited:

Board Cycle	Characteristics Members	Structural Characteristics	Role of the Board	Dominant Board Values	Characteristic Behaviors of the Board
"Founding" stage	Dedicated to the cause; morally committed	Board operates as a committee of the whole; informal & collegial	No distinction between policy & management; board acts as staff & runs the organization	Mission is a "quest"	High level of energy; maximum involvement
<Executive hired>					
"Sustaining" stage	Ownership passed to the executive	Board still operates as committee of the whole except for 1 or 2 committees; social	Not clearly defined; executive dominates	Mission still primary but not zealously so	Burned out; volunteering for organization more interesting than board work
<Crisis> (e.g., external pressure for more active board; funding threatened)					
"Super-managing" stage	Renewed commitment to mission; business-like approach emphasized	Restructuring occurs full range of committees activated	Board as program volunteers frowned on; new members recruited from middle-aged professionals	Rational processes; Participation is civic duty; board is ultimate authority	Moved to take action; high involvement; well informed

Crisis> (e.g., tension between old & new members about the role of the board; internal/external pressures)

| "Corporate" stage | Values & perspectives of professionals dominant; expect professionalism from staff; shared ownership | Committees meet regularly & report to full board; board work characterized by routine; shorter meetings with less deliberation as primarily turn to executive | To behave like a corporate board; policymaking & planning emphasized; recruit prestigious & wealthy members | Confident in its own effectiveness; mission secondary to concerns about process & structure | Rely on executive & staff input; involvement with program is avoided |

Crisis> (e.g., board members experience overcommitment in general)

| "Ratifying" stage | Socializing with other prestigious members of primary interest; academic interest in organization's cause rather than commitment | Committees only on paper; members too busy to meet | Give money & raise money; lend prestige to the organization | "No-work ethic"; procedures are an end in themselves | Low energy & involvement; knowledge of organization is limited; rubber stamps the executive's recommendations; members are bored |

Crisis>
Cycles repeated

Exhibit 1.1 Indicators of Board Behavior at Various Operational Stages

Adapted from: Miriam M. Wood, "Is Governing Board Behavior Cyclical?" *Nonprofit Management and Leadership* 3, 2 (Winter 1992: 143–150). Reprinted with permission.

Boards tend to operate according to some traditional mode and model their behavior after their immediate predecessors, because it is a known quantity. This would explain why generations of boards operate in the same cycle.

Wood's cyclical model categorizes the board behavior and attitudes that she observed in actual nonprofit organizations; it represents a small slice of reality. Excluding the founding stage, where a board needs to manage all of the affairs of a nonprofit because there is no staff, the other board cycles appear to be dysfunctional in one or more areas. For example, in the sustaining stage, the board backs away from its governance responsibilities when it passes the torch to an executive; in the supermanaging stage, boards tend to micromanage. In applying the cyclical model, a board might recognize itself operating along the lines of one or another stage.

The value of this model lies in its diagnostic potential. By examining the indicators, one can determine the stage at which a board is operating, and from that gain insight into the implications of a board's behavior.[7] If a board's way of operating becomes dysfunctional at some point in each stage, as the model implies, then the more important question is whether planned intervention might significantly alter the sequence of cycles or create yet another stage in the cycle. Organizations have turned their boards around through intervention, which suggests that it is possible to alter the duration of stages in the cycle, if not their sequence.

LEADERSHIP OR MANAGEMENT

Much has been written about leadership and the traits of a good leader; the same can be said about management and managers. However, a consensus about the qualities of a good leader or manager remains elusive: specifically, the question of whether leadership and management are equivalent or different concepts is a source of disagreement. Leadership and management *are* different, but they are not necessarily mutually exclusive. They can be distinguished by certain qualities attributable to a good leader or a good manager. Exhibit 1.2 outlines some of the contrasting characteristics of management and leadership. The chart shows that some traits of a good leader may also be found in a good manager, and vice versa. When characteristics of leaders or managers are applied to groups, it can be said that a collective body operates more in either a leadership or a management mode.

A Good *Leader:*	A Good *Manager:*
• Sees the big picture	• Focuses primarily on personnel,
• Envisions a future for the	technology, and finances
organization	• Promotes efficient and effective
• Balances opportunity with risk	work
• Motivates and inspires others	• Facilitates high-quality services
• Anticipates crises or change	• Focuses on short-term
• Is entrepreneurial	accomplishments
• Focuses primarily on mission	• Focuses on administrative activities

Exhibit 1.2   Characteristics of Leaders versus Managers

Boards as Leaders or Managers

Conventional wisdom regarding the proper role of nonprofit boards of directors states that the board sets policy and staff implements it. The board of directors provides leadership through its policy-making activities; the staff provides management through its implementation activities. This is straightforward and reasonable, and most nonprofit organizations would agree in principle with this division of responsibilities. But there are several problems with this picture.

First, this scenario presents a dichotomous relationship—boards as leaders, staff as managers—that seldom exists in reality. Instead, degrees of leadership and management may exist among boards, executives, and staffs; or boards may manage and executives lead; or boards and staffs may muddle through without real leadership from either direction. Second, organizations may need to shift the locus of leadership in response to a crisis. Third, if boards are leaders by virtue of their focus only on major policies and policy-setting activities, it must be assumed that all involved are clear about what constitutes major policy. However, that is not always true. Individuals are going to disagree over what kinds of policies are major and within the purview of board decision making. Disagreement is going to come from within the board and from the executive or staff, as individuals bring different perspectives and different experiences to the table. Fourth, adhering to the distinction between the setting and implementation of policy has implications for the board's view of executive qualifications. It implies that, in hiring an executive, a board should seek out an individual with effective management qualities. Since vision, for example, is not typically a trait of a manager, could this approach lead to nonprofits being administered by executives without vision? It does not make sense that a board would have proprietary responsibility for envisioning an organization's future or that the executive and staff could never encroach upon this domain.

Why do so many nonprofit boards tend to manage more than govern, and what difference does it make? Studies of nonprofit boards' activities and evidence drawn from board meeting agendas have shown that the topics slated for board deliberation and action are mostly related to management of the organization. Whoever sets board meeting agendas is asking the board to make decisions regarding the short-term administration of programs and services, physical resources, finances, and personnel. Instead, the board should be asked to deliberate on broader issues that may impact the organization's mission, and take action on setting explicit policies to guide the organization into the future.

For example, a board should not be asked to decide the details of facility rentals. Consider the unnecessary time and effort expended when the board of the Girls Club of Denver spent nearly an entire meeting discussing whether or not the agency should rent its facility to a community church group on Sundays, when the Club was otherwise closed. Instead of deliberating this one specific question, the board should have focused on setting a policy regarding facility use and rentals, including the qualifications of acceptable users. Eventually a policy was established, but not until after the staff became angry about rearranging furniture and equipment every Monday morning. Most boards will do what is asked of them, be it a policy decision or a management-type decision. Unfortunately, the board of the Girls Club had been asked the wrong question and did not recognize it as such.

It is easy for nonprofit boards to fall into a pattern of behaving more like managers than trustees. In prospecting for new members, boards often seek out individuals with reputations as good corporate managers, but then expect them *not* to do what they supposedly do best. It is no wonder that confusion and differences of opinion arise regarding the appropriate role of a board. Aside from unstaffed (or minimally staffed) nonprofit organizations which depend on their boards for all administrative matters, nonprofit boards become excessively involved in operational matters for several reasons:

1. Legally, a board of directors is required to perform certain administrative functions, such as authorizing signatures and approving con-

tract arrangements. It is all too easy for a board of directors to expand these authorizing functions into other areas.

2. Boards are responsible for hiring (or firing) their executives and evaluating their performance.[8] These common board responsibilities encroach on operational matters and contribute to a lack of clarity between governance and management.

3. Management is more fun than governance! Decisions about programs or services and people are more gratifying, more tangible, and comparatively easier to handle than deliberations about an unknown future and analyses of complex strategies. If an executive works part time or is on extended leave, if a board loses confidence in its executive, or if there is some other crisis, the board may take on more responsibility for day-to-day operations. But the board should step back once the organization is "stabilized," and that is sometimes difficult.

So what harm befalls an organization if its board is more oriented to management than governance? Many scholars point to a *loss of perspective* that occurs when board members become involved in trivial matters. If a board of directors and the staff are similarly engaged in operations, who is left to steer a course for the organization's future? If board members are involved with daily matters, it can be assumed that they will develop close personal relationships with staff. Intimate ties between board and staff members contributes to another kind of loss of perspective on the part of the board—its oversight role.

Another consequence may be *brain drain.* The best and brightest board members may get fed up with meetings devoted to discussions of minor issues or the constant rehashing of problems. Members brought on the board for their ability to address the big picture may stop attending meetings and later resign. Conversely, an organization's executive may get frustrated to the point of resignation when board members meddle in administrative affairs that are the responsibility of the executive. These executives may reasonably feel that their authority to manage the organization is being undermined.

Possibly the biggest potential loss to an organization whose board fails to govern is its vitality.[9] For the short term, a board that spends most of its time on operational issues is probably not dysfunctional. Over time, however, opportunities to respond to a changing environment with innovative strategies will be lost if board members' involvement in administrative details leaves them without knowledge of the organization as a whole, without the ability to see the big picture.

Assessing Nonprofit Leadership

The checklist in Exhibit 1.3 can assist boards and executives in assessing the strength of leadership in their organization. Indicators of leadership are described, followed by four questions to be answered about each indicator. This simple exercise is designed to promote a dialogue about leadership, and to encourage nonprofit boards to think about the way they govern.

Balances opportunity and risk: Is able first to focus on opportunity (the benefits to be gained) and then to weigh the risk factors (e.g., Is the decision or action reversible? What's lost if the opportunity passes?); welcomes dissent, acknowledging that hard choices are risky.

Entrepreneurial: Creates the capacity for the organization to do new things; views change as an opportunity rather than a threat.

Questions:

For each indicator, ask the following questions.

1. When was this trait demonstrated?
   Describe a recent event, decision, or other situation that demonstrates

---

Indicators of Leadership*:

Visionary: Is able to see the big picture, to consider the organization in relationship to its present and future environment, and to dream about what the organization might achieve or become.

Motivates and inspires: Is able to inspire others to want to do well and commit; emphasizes everyone's contributions to the organization.

Anticipates crises or change: Is capable of positioning the organization in a turbulent and uncertain environment to ensure equilibrium or facilitate growth; considers contingencies and alternatives a part of planning.

Mission-focused: Is focused on the primary purpose of the organization; consistently applies the question—Does this lead us closer to fulfilling our mission/goal?—to decisions and actions; constantly communicates the mission.

Exhibit 1.3 Leadership Assessment Exercise

*You do not have to use these definitions; give your own meaning to these concepts.

the leadership trait. Your answers here will disclose different perspectives that may exist about what constitutes visionary leadership, what it means to be mission-focused, and so on. For example, if there is no general consensus about what visionary leadership entails, it will be difficult for your organization to know if it has this leadership quality.

2. Who exhibited the leadership trait?

List the person or persons who demonstrated the leadership inidicator (e.g., board, executive, other staff, board and executive, all of these, other).

3. What were the circumstances?

Was it routine? Did someone rise to some occasion? Determine whether or not certain leadership qualities are always present, sometimes present, rarely shown, or never evidenced.

4. What were the implications or consequences?

Consider whether or not the response to the event, decision, or situation as described in your answers to questions 1 through 3 made a difference to the organization.

For example, if you indicated that your organization's executive has shown that he or she can motivate and inspire staff, but infrequently or only in time of crisis, then consider why that may be. Or consider how the organization would be impacted if the board exhibited the ability to consistently anticipate crises or change.

SUGGESTIONS FOR FURTHER READING

Bennis, Warren. *On Becoming A Leader.* Reading: Addison-Wesley Publishing, 1989.

Gardner, John W. *On Leadership.* New York: Free Press, 1990.

Knauft, E.B., Renee A. Berger, and Sandra T. Gray. *Profiles of Excellence: Achieving Success in the Nonprofit Sector.* San Francisco: Jossey-Bass Publishers, 1991.

Smith, David H. *Entrusted: The Moral Responsibility of Trusteeship.* Bloomington: Indiana University Press, 1995.

Zander, Alvin F. *Making Boards Effective: The Dynamics of Nonprofit Governing Boards.* San Francisco: Jossey-Bass Publishers, 1993.

CHAPTER TWO

Accountability: A Board's Fiduciary Obligations

Volunteer boards of directors are entrusted with the legal and fiduciary affairs of nonprofit corporations. *Fiduciary* is a legal term referring to an individual or individuals in whom property or power is entrusted for the benefit of another. State laws recognize this position of trust and, to varying degrees, regulate its fulfillment. In some states the laws regulating charitable and nonprofit corporations are mainly registration and reporting acts. In other states, laws attempt to define the ethical responsibilities connected with the solicitation and management of charitable funds. Some offer immunity from civil liability to nonprofit board members. This chapter demonstrates that membership on the board of directors of a nonprofit organization should not be taken lightly, and presents a basic overview of accountability and of the legal and moral obligations of a nonprofit board of directors.

ACCOUNTABILITY ISSUES

Accountability means responsibility to someone or for something. In the case of an organization, the "someone" refers to stakeholders, those who have an interest in the group's success because they will be affected by its outcomes. They may include staff, board members, beneficiaries or clients, competitors, donors, neighbors, suppliers, the general public, and so forth. They share in the ownership of an organization to varying degrees; those closest to the organization, such as staff, board members, clients, and donors, have a greater stake in whatever happens to the organization and are considered primary stakeholders. It is up to each nonprofit organization to (1) identify its primary and secondary stakeholders, (2) determine its degree of accountability to them, and (3) decide to what extent its activities will be reported to them.

Accountability extracts a price. The time spent preparing reports and making presentations to community groups or other stakeholders is time away from running programs. In the public sector, administrators of large agencies have complained that their effectiveness as managers is actually hampered by legislative oversight.[1] Certainly, nonprofit executives such as hospital administrators and presidents of colleges and universities must feel constrained as they continually consult with various segments of the public with legitimate concerns about their institutions' operations.

The "something" in the definition of accountability could refer to a program, a treatment modality, a method of teaching/training, or a general way of conducting business. An accountable organization takes responsibility for the consequences of its choices, such as selection of a solution to some problem. An organization's actions affect people related both directly and indirectly to a problem. For example, when a church in an upper-middle-class neighborhood decided to use a portion of its facility as a temporary shelter for homeless persons, it became responsible for consequences to the homeless (those directly related to the problem), and to its neighbors (those indirectly related). From the perspective of the homeless, the suburban location of the church facility was inaccessible. For the church's neighbors, a shelter for the homeless in their neighborhood was unacceptable; they perceived that it would devalue their property and feared for their personal safety. This church made a decision to help alleviate a problem but seemingly failed to consider the consequences of the solution.

Board and Executive Accountability

Each member of an organization is responsible for his or her own behavior, work, and compliance with the rules of the organization. Supervisors, by virtue of their position, are held accountable for the behavior, work, and compliance of those under them. Thus accountability accumulates and flows upward to the top of the organization—to the chief executive. In turn, executives report to their boards and boards hold executives accountable for their behavior, work, and compliance, as well as that of the staff. If staff are allowed to go directly to the board for whatever reason, the lines of responsibility become muddied. This undesirable condition is called *leaky accountability* because the source of responsibility is difficult to trace.[2]

Type	Description	Mechanism
Managerial	Responsibility for running the organization efficiently and effectively	Internal audits; fiscal control policies; employee performance evaluations
Political	External controls imposed through contracting relationships (e.g., United Way, government grants)	Data collections and record-keeping (e.g., numbers of clients served and demographics, project fund accounting)

Exhibit 2.1   Types of Accountability and Mechanisms for Implementation

The nonprofit board of directors has the highest level of accountability because of its unique ownership and stakeholder position. In addition to the formal, legal ownership of the organization, a board also has moral ownership based on its social obligation to act as steward of the nonprofit's health and welfare. Because of its moral ownership, a board is accountable for *integrity of governance,* or organizational performance.[3] (Chapter 8 discusses a board's role in evaluation.)

Exhibit 2.1 illustrates other types of accountability, and different mechanisms for implementing accountability.

Board members, the executive, and key management staff should at all times be able to identify the primary sources of accountability for themselves and their organization. An accountability assessment should be included in an organization's evaluation. Exhibit 2.2 provides an account-

Stakeholders	Reporting Mechanism	Frequency (Minimum)
Primary:		
staff	meetings and memos	weekly
board	meetings and reports	monthly
donors	annual report	yearly
contractors	audits and program reports	quarterly
Secondary:		
general community	oral presentations	yearly
competitors	conferences/networking	quarterly

Exhibit 2.2   Accountability Checklist

ability checklist, with a breakdown of stakeholders, reporting mechanisms, and desired frequency of reports. Preparation of such a checklist could be a starting point for discussion about organizational accountability.

LEGAL ISSUES AND OBLIGATIONS

The Foundations of a Nonprofit's Operation

There are three documents basic to a nonprofit organization's operations: the articles of incorporation, the bylaws, and the Internal Revenue Service (IRS) Letter of Determination. The articles of incorporation creating an organization are typically filed with the secretary of state's office in the state in which an organization is located. State laws on nonprofit corporations specify the provisions that must be included in this document. If a charitable organization plans to seek recognition of tax-exempt status under Internal Revenue Code Section 501(c)(3), its articles must include additional information regarding its qualifying tax-exempt purpose.

Every incorporated nonprofit organization should have bylaws, a document that outlines the rules governing the organization's operations. Since this document can have important legal ramifications, a board should ensure that its bylaws are written with care and thereafter reviewed regularly. Bylaws are the rule book for a board of directors; they guide directors in their transactions on behalf of the organization, and they may contain any provisions pertinent to managing the nonprofit corporation (within the constraints of the law). The most common bylaw provisions address:

- members (if applicable)
- meetings of members
- voting of members and quorums
- the board of directors (number of members, terms, vacancies, etc.)
- committees of the board
- officers of the board
- provisions for adopting and amending the bylaws.

A nonprofit's third basic document is its IRS Letter of Determination, which describes the category of exemption granted to the organization. Not every nonprofit elects to file for tax exemption, because there are some disadvantages in doing so (e.g., record-keeping and reporting requirements, limits on certain activities). Churches and religious organizations need not file for tax-exempt status unless they also provide nonreligious services (e.g., child care, social services). Most eligible nonprofits find that the advantages of filing for exemption under IRS Section 501(c)(3) far outweigh the disadvantages. The benefits of tax exemption include:

1. exemption from federal corporate income tax on earnings related to an organization's "exempt purpose"
2. exemption from property and sales tax, in most states
3. exemption from federal unemployment tax
4. deductibility of contributions by the donor, which can boost an organization's fund-raising efforts
5. eligibility for foundation and government grants, which require recipients to be tax exempt.[4]

There are many categories of tax-exempt organizations in addition to 501(c)(3) "charitable" organizations, from labor unions to social clubs; different rules apply to the various categories. (See the list of tax-exempt organizations in Appendix A.) The IRS laws governing nonprofit corporations are complex; organizations are wise to seek expert counsel for their initial filing or for requesting a change of tax-exempt status. The Suggestions for Further Reading section at the end of this chapter includes references on nonprofit tax planning and compliance, and on forming a nonprofit corporation.

A Board's Legal Responsibilities and Liabilities

In agreeing to serve on the board of a nonprofit, a member should be prepared to attend to the affairs of the corporate body and devote energy to fulfilling the responsibilities of this position of trust. Because legal responsibilities and liabilities are inherent to board membership, members must take their roles seriously.

State laws on nonprofit corporations impose certain "standards of care" on boards of directors. For example, the following quotation from the Seattle–King County Bar Association is in their booklet on how to form a nonprofit corporation in the state of Washington:

A director must perform his or her duties as a member of the board and as a committee member "in good faith," in a manner such director believes to be in the best interests of the corporation, and with such care, including reasonable inquiry, as an ordinarily prudent person in a like position would use under similar circumstances.[5]

In carrying out their duties, and under these standards of care, directors also are expected to carefully review and evaluate information (e.g., financial statements) before making decisions; prudently manage the organization's resources; ensure the safety of the corporation's legal documents; and act in a professional manner. While not prohibited, certain actions—such as conflicts of interest and self-dealing on the part of board members—are usually subject to strict scrutiny.

When board members act in good faith and in the best interests of the nonprofit corporation, they are generally protected from personal liability for any errors in judgment. If a nonprofit is sued, in most cases the organization itself is the defendant rather than individuals. However unusual, there is still the potential for individual board members or officers and key staff persons to be named in a lawsuit. Therefore, boards should take steps to limit their liability by having an indemnification clause in their bylaws and purchasing directors' and officers' (D&O) liability insurance (also called "errors and omissions" insurance). Such insurance is important for any organization with responsibility for managing personnel and funds, and especially for organizations involved with housing or property management. *Indemnification* means that the organization will pay, within reason, any expenses or liability incurred by a director of the board (or staff covered under this policy) who is involved because of his or her position with the organization. D&O insurance protects board members and officers in their roles as decisionmakers.[6] In some states, the officers and executives of nonprofit organizations are granted immunity from civil liability under certain conditions. (See Florida's statute on immunity from civil liability in Appendix B.)

There are ways for individual board members to minimize personal liability. Because it is critical for board members to be informed, regular attendance at board meetings, as well as perusal of pertinent materials, is important. In addition, board members must be constantly aware that they are fiduciaries for the organization and are therefore obligated to behave prudently. Board members also should:

- understand the organization's legal form and structure
- know the organization's operations—its programs, clients, and so on
- understand the organization's administrative systems

- ask questions
- read books and articles related to governance of nonprofits for further understanding of nonprofit boards' roles and responsibilities and nonprofit organizations' operations.[7]

Nonprofit board members are accountable to their constituents, and the general public has a right to expect these board members to behave competently and with diligence.

Regulations

Because tax-exempt status is critical to most nonprofit organizations, boards should be aware of regulatory issues that might endanger that status for their organizations. It is equally important to be alert to the mood of governments regarding charitable exemptions.

Despite recently escalating complaints about excessive government regulation, nonprofit organizations have generally escaped close government scrutiny. However, as all levels of government are being forced to look for additional sources of revenue, some of the tax-exempt benefits enjoyed by charitable organizations are becoming popular targets for reform. State and local governments claim to forfeit millions of dollars each year in property taxes because of large holdings by tax-exempt colleges and universities, churches, hospitals, and other nonprofit institutions. Increasingly, states are challenging rules of tax exemption for nonprofit organizations. The following two examples point to the kinds of challenges nonprofits are experiencing:

In June 1991, Dayton Art Institute's museum shop had to fight to keep its exemption from property tax. The Ohio Board of Tax Appeals questioned whether the museum shop's framing service duplicated and unfairly competed with commercial services. The Board eventually ruled that the shop's services were unique and did not duplicate commercial ventures because it also promoted art education.

In July 1992, Pennsylvania's Commonwealth Court upheld the denial of property-tax exemption for three Wayne County summer camps that provided religious education to children. The camps failed to meet one of the state's four tests for determining whether an organization is a public charity: It did not "relieve a government burden."

The camps were unable to prove that the government had an obligation to provide education, social, or recreational activities for children during the summer months.

The closer a nonprofit's activities resemble a for-profit competitor, or the
more visible an institution, the greater the chance for scrutiny of its tax-
exempt purpose.

Licensing

A board need not know the specifics of all licensing requirements for its
organization. However, to fulfill its oversight role, a board should at least
know that the organization is in compliance with all applicable statutory
requirements.

Licensing is another form of regulation that enables the government to
supervise the operations of nonprofit organizations. Because licensing is
also a source of revenue for local governments, nonprofits should expect
more rather than fewer licensing requirements and should plan for periodic increases in licensing fees. Some activities of nonprofit organizations
that require a license or a permit include the following:

- *Ticket sales.* Certain information, such as pricing and liability, must be
  printed on a ticket to a public event. When an organization uses an
  external agent, such as a ticket outlet, other liabilities are incurred and
  additional regulations may apply.
- *Food services.* Incidental food sales on an organization's premises to
  its own members or constituents (e.g., vending machines, a camp can-
  teen) rarely require special licensing. If food sales involve meal prepa-
  rations and are available to the general public (e.g., a museum cafe),
  or involve government funding, local health department licensing is
  usually necessary. However, a church that prepares and serves a free
  meal for the homeless on Thanksgiving typically does not require licensing. When in doubt, it is best to consult the local health department.
- *Serving alcohol.* Serving alcohol at organizational functions is first a
  matter of policy. Many nonprofit boards have established policies
  prohibiting alcohol on their organizations' premises under any circumstances. If alcohol is sold at an occasional function, local liquor licensing regulations may require a temporary permit; if alcohol is sold

on a regular basis (e.g., wine at theater intermissions), different licensing may be required.

- *Mailings.* A nonprofit organization can take advantage of special postal rates for bulk mailing. A mailing permit is required; certain rules for preparing mailings must be followed, and these rules often change.

There are other mandatory areas of licensing from which nonprofit organizations are not exempt (e.g., building permits and permits for boxing, wrestling, and other amateur athletic competitions). The more clinical the nature of an organization's services (e.g., physical rehabilitation, research), the more likely the need for licensing. For some types of organizations, starting up program operations is contingent upon obtaining statutory approval in advance.

Finally, as with any other organization, a nonprofit must conform to the laws and regulations of the Equal Employment Opportunity Commission (EEOC) with regard to human resources policies and practices. Key staff and board members should be familiar with the various types of illegal discrimination, know the consequences of violating the spirit and letter of the laws of the EEOC, and be aware of all regulations affecting their responsibilities as an employer. Exhibit 2.3 summarizes the major EEOC laws.

Trouble Spots and Red Flags

Nonprofit organizations should be concerned about legislation that affects charitable giving and activities in their field, as well as other referendum issues. The issues of lobbying, unrelated business income, and regulations pertaining to fund-raising are particularly sensitive areas.

Lobbying. The IRS defines *lobbying* as carrying on propaganda, or otherwise attempting to influence legislation. Any direct or indirect effort by a 501(c)(3) organization to support or oppose a referendum may be construed by the IRS as lobbying. There are two types of lobbying:

- *Direct lobbying* includes the presentation of testimony at public hearings held by legislative committees, correspondence and meetings with legislators and their staffs, and publication of documents advocating specific legislative action.
- *Grassroots* lobbying consists of appeals to the general public, or segments of the general public, to contact legislators or to take other specific action with regard to legislative matters.[8]

Law	Description
Equal Pay Act of 1963	Prohibits wage discrimination on basis of sex
Title VII—Civil Rights Act of 1964 (amended 1972, 1991)	Prohibits discrimination in the conditions of employment on basis of race, color, sex, religion, or national origin—also covers sexual harassment
Pregnancy Discrimination Act of 1978	Prohibits employee benefits discrimination based on pregnancy
Age Discrimination in Employment Act of 1967 (amended 1978)	Prohibits discrimination in the conditions of employment based on age (40 years or older)
Older Workers Benefit Protection Act of 1990	Prohibits benefit plan discrimination based on age
Immigration Reform and Control Act of 1986	Prohibits discrimination based on citizenship or national origin (hiring illegal aliens prohibited)
Americans With Disabilities Act of 1991	Prohibits discrimination on basis of physical or mental handicap

Exhibit 2.3   Major EEOC Laws Applicable to All Employees

Charitable organizations are not prohibited from either type of lobbying, but the IRS carefully scrutinizes an organization's expenditures, time, and influence in such efforts. Some nonprofit organizations [501(c)(4)s or 501(c)(3)s under Section 501(h)] are organized explicitly for the purpose of influencing legislation. For these organizations, compliance with IRS tax-exempt regulations requires that they limit their total lobbying expenditures to a certain percentage of total exempt-purpose expenditures. These limitations, set forth in Public Law 94-455, should be thoroughly researched by nonprofits that lobby or those considering it. In summary, boards must pay attention to lobbying and legislative activities and their related costs, and ask for a regular accounting in order to avoid tax penalties. When in doubt, an organization should secure professional counsel.

It is also better for a nonprofit to avoid certain other kinds of actions that can be construed as political campaign activities. For example, an arts organization needed the financial support of the county council for a major capital project. The chief executive of this organization felt very strongly about supporting one particular council candidate's election bid, presumably because the candidate supported the organization's project. The executive wrote a letter on the agency's letterhead to all of the board members asking them to attend a fund-raising event for this candidate. The board chair immediately redressed the executive, requested that she write a memo for the personnel file stating that the letter had been sent in error, and requested repayment of the postage and stationery costs incurred by the agency. The board's concern was partly one of ethics and partly of appearance, but the greater risk was that the tax-exempt status of the organization could have been jeopardized.

Unrelated business income. A nonprofit organization is taxed on its *unrelated business income,* defined as income generated from activities substantially unrelated to an organization's tax-exempt purpose. This tax is intended to eliminate unfair competition with for-profit businesses and has been a provision of federal regulation since 1950. Its significance is felt more today, as an increasing number of nonprofit organizations are turning to entrepreneurial activities to support the costs of running their programs. A nonprofit organization can operate business activities if they further the organization's tax-exempt purpose. The frequency of a business activity can affect its classification as taxable. For example, an occasional bingo game sponsored by a nonprofit organization would be a fund-raising event. However, the proceeds from regularly scheduled bingo games are considered unrelated business income and are taxable.

The conduct of incidental unrelated business activities is not cause for the loss of a nonprofit organization's tax-exempt status. However, the IRS can target for taxation some revenue-generating aspect of an otherwise exempt activity. For example, an organization may publish a newsletter that furthers its tax-exempt purpose by informing the public about its services. If the newsletter is sold, the income from subscriptions is usually nontaxable. However, if the newsletter carries paid ads, the advertising income may be taxed even if it only produces revenue equal to the cost of publication.

Some business-related activities clearly do not jeopardize their organization's tax status, such as a thrift shop that sells donated goods, is run entirely by volunteers, and whose proceeds wholly support the purpose of a charitable, tax-exempt organization. The earnings from any investments made by a nonprofit organization are not considered business income; the courts have ruled that investing is not a business activity in a tax context. Also, businesses conducted primarily for the convenience of an organization's constituents or employees (e.g., a hospital's cafeteria) are called "substantially related activities" and are usually not taxed.

Fund-raising activities.   Some state and local governments regulate fund-raising activities. The more common statutes governing solicitation activities deal with the issues of disclosure of fund-raising costs, limits on fund-raising expenditures relative to the amount raised by a third party, and licensing for public fund-raising appeals (e.g., street-corner collections, door-to-door campaigns). Laws regulating disclosure may require a nonprofit charitable organization to provide donors and potential donors with certain types of information. In most instances, a brief statement is acceptable, provided it is printed on donors' receipts with a notation that complete information can be obtained by contacting the organization at a specified address and phone number. The state agencies usually responsible for regulation of charitable solicitation include secretary of state offices, attorney general offices, and departments of consumer affairs.

One area of the tax law that is puzzling to many nonprofit organizations deals with deductions for deferred gifts or gifts of transferred property and other noncash donations. Most nonprofits need not concern themselves with these complex regulations which primarily affect the donor. However, someone in an organization actively engaged in building an endowment fund (either a board member or development staff) should have a working knowledge of capital gains and estate taxes in order to talk with potential donors of large sums. Overall, it is in everyone's best interest to advise such potential donors to consult their own accountants or attorneys.

ETHICAL OBLIGATIONS

In January 1995, the state of Washington passed a very strict ethics bill. When one member of the Washington State Transportation Commission was asked about the impact of the new code on public boards such as hers, she replied:

> We've become very cautious about behaving scrupulously. For example, commissioners like myself used to be guests at the Apple Cup.[9] Now, even if I am the guest speaker at a luncheon I buy my own lunch. The real dilemma is that I am no longer free to speak out on ballot issues. It's really too bad when an informed group can't advocate what they know best. So, in some respects the new code may be too strict but with any legislative reform, not everything is done well. Overall it is better to have [the ethics code] than not.[10]

Public outcry over fraud, waste, and abuse in the government sector over the past decade has prompted states such as Washington to initiate codes of ethics. However, government is not the only sector of society responding to the public's raised level of consciousness. Business and nonprofit organizations are increasingly aware that actively promoting ethical behavior and practices not only makes sense from a customer-relations standpoint, but also represents a better way to run a business.

While accountability is easily understood as a matter of responsibility, ethics is a more slippery concept. It refers to matters of morality, questions of right and wrong, and is contingent upon an individual's perspective. One United Way board member feels that the biggest ethical problem among nonprofit organizations is discrimination on the basis of gender or sexual preference. She said that some organizations define who they serve by *exclusion* and that this is wrong. Illegal discrimination based on gender or sexual preference pertains to employment practices and certain commercial transactions. It may not be politically correct or ethical, but it is not illegal for a private organization to designate who they want to serve. Many institutions (e.g., the Citadel, the U.S. military) are coming under increasing pressure to change their policies regarding gender or sexual preference.

Other organizations have found ways to either integrate or reconcile their private beliefs with an *open-door policy* service mission. For example, the Salvation Army takes what they call a "biblical stance" regarding homosexual behavior:

> Homosexual behavior . . . promoted and accepted as an alternative life style, is contrary to the teachings of the Bible and presents a serious threat to the integrity and solidarity of society as a whole. We believe, however, that we should seek, in the spirit of Jesus Christ, to understand and help the homosexual, differentiating between homosexual acts and the innate tendency which may or may not lead to that activity.[11]

Because the Salvation Army is also "concerned with the spiritual and social needs of all people," they do not exclude homosexuals from the benefits of their social welfare services.

Ethical behavior is more complicated than beliefs about right or wrong. Whereas "ethics involves substantive reasoning about obligations, consequences, and ultimate ends," ethical behavior "involves thinking more systematically about values which are embedded in the choices we make." [12] Boards and executives should examine and question the standards upon which their decisions are made. Standards reflect current societal thinking about what is right and wrong; this changes over time as new societal concerns emerge. Additionally, the administrative decisions of nonprofit organizations typically involve making hard choices between scarce and competing resources; these are value-laden decisions that invoke moral principles.

Making ethical decisions can be a real dilemma for executives and boards of directors. When asked to describe the types of ethical issues that her board has encountered, one board chairperson said:

> Ethics is hard to define, perhaps it is feeling discomfort about something. For our theater group, it could be related to what is being produced on stage. Because our organization values diversity, some of our productions are controversial; but the board has refrained from acting as censors. However, if the artistic director were to repeatedly produce plays in bad taste, the board would probably fire him.[13]

A board should provide leadership in establishing standards of conduct and ethical parameters for carrying out the organization's mission. It does this through the executive by setting limits on and generally defining behavioral expectations of the executive's position. Because boards are comprised of individuals with different sets of values, it is difficult to establish policies to address specific ethical situations. Instead, a board of directors should strive for consensus about ethical and prudent behavior. It may begin with a broad policy statement such as, "the chief executive may neither cause nor allow organizational practice that is imprudent or unethical."[14] Albeit simplistic, this statement says that the board is concerned about ethical behavior and practices and that ethics is part of the organization's culture. From a broad policy statement, a board may proceed to define what it feels are the limits of acceptability regarding treatment of clients, relationships with donors, fund-raising practices, and so forth. The Hospice of the Florida Suncoast is one nonprofit organization that has met this responsibility and created a "Code of Organizational Ethics" (see Appendix C).

A board of directors and executive set the tone for ethical organizational behavior in myriad ways. For example:

- Does the board avoid giving an honest appraisal of the executive's performance in fear of reprisal from a civil lawsuit?
- Does the organization accept funds from corporations or individuals whose business practices are questionable?

Instructions: For each question check the number that in your opinion best applies to your organization—where 1 is *yes*, 2 is *maybe* or *sometimes*, 3 is *no*, and 4 is *don't know*.

Note: These are only suggestions to get you started. Organizations will want to design their own sets of questions tailored to their own unique circumstances and reflecting their missions.

POLICY   1 2 3 4

1. Does your organization have written policies? If not, proceed to the next section; if so, answer the following questions.
2. Do policies include words like *honesty, integrity, responsibility,* and *accountability,* or other positive value statements?
3. Do policies contain language that is proscriptive and threatening, with an emphasis on punishment for noncompliance?
4. Does your organization have a policy addressing standards of behavior or conduct?
5. If *no* to number 4, does your organization handle issues of ethics informally by peer pressure, or through organizational norms?

OPERATIONS   1 2 3 4

6. Are employees generally considered to be fair and honest:
   By clients?
   By coworkers?
   By the executive or top management?
7. Do organizational procedures discourage fraud, waste, and abuse?
8. Do organizational procedures encourage disclosure of abuse?
9. Are confidentiality mechanisms in place for *whistle-blowers?*
10. Are value-oriented statements included:
    In employees' performance appraisals?
    In the organization's program evaluations?
11. Does management encourage discussion of ethical issues/questions in staff meetings?
12. Do hiring practices include consideration of an individual's moral character or ethical behavior?
13. Are ethical implications a part of discussions about contracted services, collaborations, or other interorganizational arrangements?

Exhibit 2.4 Framework for an Ethics Audit

- Does the board approve budgets that have been padded?
- To what extent does the executive encourage or discourage whistle-blowing?
- Are employees encouraged to practice confidentiality with respect to their clients, or are clients' problems a matter of office gossip?

Those in leadership positions should ensure that an ethics audit is conducted to determine if ethical decision making and behavior is sustained and promoted by the organization. Exhibit 2.4 provides a sample of such an audit. The audit mechanism is less important than the initiation of some process for examining and discussing ethical issues. The discovery of the values of an organization's members can be enlightening. More importantly, those discoveries need to be analyzed and acted upon to determine (1) the cause(s) of ethical or unethical conduct in certain situations, (2) specific recommendations to encourage ethical behavior or correct unethical behavior, (3) courses of action, and (4) responsibility for implementation. Because ethical issues are emotionally charged and may produce conflict during discussion, use of a consultant may facilitate an ethics audit.

It has been only within the past thirty years that the majority of states have adopted a common definition of nonprofit charitable organizations, including the duties and powers of their boards of directors. However, considerable disagreement apparently remains among states as to the place of tax-exempt charitable organizations in society and the rights, powers, and obligations of their trustees.[15] Federal and state regulations aimed at charitable organizations are becoming more common, and boards of directors are affected as the nature and extent of their liability is altered. A board's legal and moral responsibility to behave in a prudent manner obligates it to keep current on changes in the legal and regulatory environment affecting nonprofit organizations, as well as to maintain high ethical standards.

SUGGESTIONS FOR FURTHER READING

Blazek, Jody, CPA. *Tax & Financial Planning for Tax-Exempt Organizations: Forms, Checklists, Procedures.* New York: John Wiley & Sons, 1990.

Committee on Values and Ethics. *Ethics and the Nation's Voluntary and Philanthropic Community.* Washington, D.C.: Independent Sector, 1991.

Lewis, Carol W. *The Ethics Challenge in Public Service.* San Francisco: Jossey-Bass Publishers, 1991.

Nicholas, Ted. The Complete Guide to Nonprofit Corporations. Dearborn: Enterprise Publications, 1993.

State Tax Trends for Nonprofits is a quarterly newsletter prepared by the law firm of Harmon, Curran, Gallagher & Spielberg for the Independent Sector. For information on this publication, contact: Harmon, Curran, Gallagher & Spielberg; 2001 S St., NW, suite 430; Washington, D.C., 20009; 202/328-3500. Or, contact Independent Sector at 1828 L St., NW; Washington, D.C., 20036.

CHAPTER THREE

Structuring a Board for Maximum Effectiveness

Anonprofit board's ability to effectively shape policy and further the organization's mission is either enhanced or constrained by the way its members relate to one another; and a board's organization and structure defines how members will interact. Taking the time to evaluate board structure can avoid repetitions of dysfunctional patterns that might lead to a crisis. The following criteria should be considered in evaluating board structure.

- Simplicity in structure is better.
- Board structure should create unity among members rather than separation and compartmentalization.[1]
- The structure should support an orderly flow of work; areas of responsibility should be clear.
- Reporting procedures and procedures for managing input should be established; committees should collect data/information (input) and report this input at full meetings of the board.
- Board structure should support timely transmission of information.
- Inactive members defeat the collective purpose of a board.

Because each nonprofit organization is unique, there is no right way to organize a nonprofit board of directors; flexibility and adaptability are key factors. A governing body must reflect changes in an organization in order to remain effective. The following examples demonstrate that there are different structures of nonprofit boards and different reasons behind those structures.

35

- For over thirty years, a Colorado Council of Boy Scouts has had a board of approximately seventy-five members. While that may sound cumbersome, it works for them and has evolved into a sophisticated structure of two boards—an associate board of about forty-six members, and a board of trustees with about twenty-seven members.

- Reorganization of a passive Rescue Mission board started several years ago with a new executive director who demanded changes. After five years of deliberate culling and consolidation, a working board emerged that was committed to helping the agency better serve the community.

- The Board of Trustees of Craig Rehabilitation Hospital created a separate foundation board nearly a decade ago in an effort to meet the financial needs of the institution.

This chapter examines board structure, the issue of diversity in board composition, and supportive structures that can help a board better fulfill its obligations.

BOARD SIZE

Demographics of Board Size

The National Center for Nonprofit Boards (NCNB), headquartered in Washington, D.C., conducted a nationwide survey on nonprofit boards in 1994. A purposive sample of approximately 5,000 nonprofit organizations was drawn, 95 percent with annual revenues of at least $100,000. The 1,163 organizations who responded to the survey represented a broad range of nonprofits: human services (41 percent), health (18 percent), education (12 percent), arts and culture (8 percent), religious (3 percent), professional (3 percent), environment (2 percent), international (1 percent), trade (1 percent), and others (14 percent).[2]

The NCNB survey showed that the larger the budget of an organization, the larger its board of directors. Of those organizations with annual revenues in excess of $1 million, 40 percent to 46 percent had more than twenty members on their boards. In contrast, only 18 percent to 26 percent of organizations with estimated annual revenues from $99,999 to $249,999 had boards with more than twenty members.[3] Other variables, such as the mission of the organization and field, showed no correlation to board size.

Board sizes ranged from a low of one to five members (1 percent), to forty-one members and more (4 percent). The median was seventeen, and the average board had nineteen members. The majority of nonprofit organizations (65 percent) reported boards of eleven to twenty-five members. Interestingly, religious organizations had the highest average number of board members (24.27), followed by international organizations (23.67), and arts and cultural organizations (22.97). Trade associations (16.55) and health-care organizations (17.16) averaged the smallest boards.[4]

The Issue of Board Size

The size of any nonprofit board of directors should reflect the nature and mission of the organization. There is a strong correlation between size and effective functioning: "There are numerous examples of problems at both extremes [too small or too large]. Although skillful leadership and careful management of board affairs can mitigate these problems, there is no escaping the fact that size [of a board] itself matters greatly." [5]

Just as important as the number of members on a board is the *perception* of size. Studies such as the one outlined in the previous section report a range in board sizes or an average size. However, some may feel that a board with thirty-six members is a big board while others might consider it a medium-sized board. For purposes of comparison, the following discussion of board size uses these definitions:

- small board: twelve or fewer members
- medium-sized board: thirteen to thirty members
- large board: more than thirty members.

One purpose of a large board of directors is maximum participation, based on the argument that there are greater opportunities for solving community problems when interaction among many different constituencies occurs. Proponents of large governing bodies state that size contributes to democratic decision making. A large number of people representing a broad range of perspectives can contribute different ideas and alternatives to arrive at resolutions more responsive to, and representative of, the needs of the organization's constituency. For example, the boards of national organizations are often large because they need proportional representation from different groups affected by the decisions and policies made at the national level. Brian O'Connell, past president of Independent Sector, once said that the maximum number is approximately one hundred members: "Beyond that, participation isn't significant enough to create a feeling of honor and responsibility." [6]

Some nonprofits establish a large board to create a sphere of influence. The thirty-five-member board of a Girl Scouts organization has, in effect, thirty-five different points of access. This board is composed mainly of business leaders but also includes educators, professionals, and other civic leaders. The chief executive knows her board has access to help if there is some problem or particular need in a scouting district. For example, when the agency wants publicity for some event, certain board members have access to the media and to advertising and public relations firms. When bids for capital improvements on scouting facilities are needed, the board turns to members with access to architects, contractors, and building material suppliers.

Opponents argue that it is impossible for large boards to function effectively as a single entity. Work must be parceled out to committees; the full board becomes a rubber stamp to committee work. Interaction and collegiality are lost except at the committee level.[7] At a meeting of a large board, it is easier for members to hide their lack of preparation, allow others to take responsibility for discussion, or defer on difficult issues. Regardless of size, boards must weed out inattentive members or those who do not represent relevant constituencies; this is particularly problematic with large boards, which tend to add more members to compensate for ineffective ones. Setting limits on terms of office is one way to accomplish this goal.

The way nonprofit organizations have traditionally recruited boards of directors has contributed to producing medium-sized boards. When a nonprofit forms its board, a common practice is to fill board seats according to what committees need to be staffed. Most boards have five or six standing committees. (See NCNB survey results on board committees in Chapter 4.) Excluding the executive committee because it is comprised of officers and sometimes committee chairpersons, if each committee were expected to have three to five members, then twelve to twenty-five board members would be needed to staff all of the committees. Add one to five additional members to this core group because they have a special expertise or represent an important constituency, and the result is a medium-sized board of thirteen to thirty members. There are no particular advantages or disadvantages to medium-sized boards. Criticism of board size tends to focus on the extremes.

Small boards are based on the principle of the few: Growth in size brings about a disproportionate increase in complexity as well as specialization, which in turn leads to the estrangement of individual participants. Another assumption is that too many opinions only confuse the discussion of issues and muddle decision making; thus, a small decision-making body can be more effective. Even organizations with medium-sized or large boards may actually operate on the principle of a few by relying heavily on an executive committee. To illustrate an extreme, the board of directors of a private alternative school in Denver has two members—the founding director and his wife. Two members do not constitute a board; in this case the board exists simply to fulfill the legal incorporation requirements. An advisory body, comprised of parents, assists in formulating policies.

One problem with a small board of directors is that members' backgrounds, experiences, and perspectives may be insufficiently diverse; *group think* (conformity to one perspective) is more likely to occur, which can inhibit creative decision making. (See discussion on decision making in Chapter 7.) Because small groups tend to rely on one to three strong individuals to provide leadership and momentum, they typically lack depth. On a practical note, regardless of board size, it is always hard to find meeting times that guarantee 100% attendance. This is especially problematic for smaller boards, which may be unable to make decisions because of a lack of a quorum, or may have to make decisions based on minimal input. Finally, if there are fewer members to share in the work of the board, burnout can result, causing a high turnover of members.

THE COMPOSITION OF BOARDS

The composition of nonprofit boards has changed over time. Boards have become more inclusive of politically organized constituencies such as women and people of color.[8] This change has been attributed in part to government's financial support of the nonprofit sector. Nonprofits involved in service contracting with the government have been influenced by public-sector norms of representativeness and inclusiveness. Additionally, government-imposed accountability measures for organizations receiving federal funds have influenced board composition; boards are expected to function as leaders in the community and represent specific constituencies. Another reason for the changes in board composition is that nonprofits are serving broader, more diverse constituencies.[9] The shift in client demographics has been an incentive for some organizations to make a greater commitment to inclusiveness.

Diversity refers to differences across a range of demographic attributes. Many people think of diversity only in terms of ethnicity, gender, and age. But it also refers to less visible attributes such as religion, national origin, physical and mental ability, socioeconomic background, level of education, and marital and family status. Organizations evolve through several stages of multicultural development: acquisition of knowledge, establishment of awareness and sensitivity, and appreciation of the value of diversity.[10]

While positive changes in the diversity of nonprofit boards have occurred, this evolution is not yet complete. Baseline data from which to compare specific gains in diversity is lacking, but two surveys of data on nonprofit boards are telling. In 1992, the NCNB commissioned a nationwide assessment of nonprofit board diversity. The findings, summarized in Exhibit 3.1, showed that nonprofit boards were dominated by members classified as White/Caucasian.

The majority of the respondents to the 1992 diversity survey (71 percent) felt it was important to have a culturally diverse board of directors, but only 36.3 percent had a diversity policy in place. In the survey, 90 percent of respondents indicated that the biggest obstacle to diversity was a (mistaken) belief that diversity was not needed because the people served were not diverse, 89 percent indicated that the organization's mission and goals did not require diversity, and 79 percent indicated a lack of awareness of the importance of diversity among staff and board members.[11]

The results of NCNB's 1994 survey and profile of nonprofit boards were consistent with their 1992 survey. Nonprofit boards were still comprised

---

The following are some characteristics and average numbers for boards with an average of twenty-one members:

Characteristic	Average Number
White/Caucasian	16.7
Black/African American	2.1
Hispanic/Latino	.7
Native American	.1
Asian American/Pacific Islander	.3
Female	8.5
Elderly (65 years and over)	1.8
Disabled	.5
Homosexual	.6
Young (under 21 years)	1.0
Organization's Consumers/Clients	7.0

Exhibit 3.1   Indicators of Board Diversity

Source: Jennifer M. Rutledge, *Building Board Diversity* (Washington, D.C.: National Center for Nonprofit Boards, 1994), 44. Reprinted with permission.

primarily of White/Caucasian males and middle-aged individuals. Exhibit 3.2 displays NCNB's most recent data on selected characteristics of board members. Despite some recent progress, it is obvious that more must be done to raise awareness of the importance of board diversity.

Building A Diverse Board

The move toward organizational diversity must begin with commitment and open-mindedness. It also requires explicit policies, training and accountability measures, and treatment as an ongoing process rather than a goal to be met and then set aside. The board chairperson plays a key role in creating a climate for change, and in motivating and supporting members in their efforts. An organization's executive needs to generally support the board's diversity-building, providing direct assistance only if asked to undertake specific tasks, such as the recommendation of diversity trainers and consultants. An executive who has developed a broad-based community network could also assist in identifying prospective new board members.

The NCNB has outlined a process and strategy for developing an initiative on board diversity. The four phases of this process are:

- planning
- building awareness
- taking action
- evaluation.[12]

Ethnic Composition		Gender Composition		Composition by Age	
White/Caucasian	86%	Male	54%	Under 30 years	3%
Hispanic/Latino	3%	Female	46%	30–39 years	18%
Black/African American	9%			40–49 years	34%
Asian American	1%			50–59 years	27%
Other	1%			60–69 years	14%
				70 years and older	5%

Exhibit 3.2   Composition of Nonprofit Boards of Directors (1994)

Source: Larry H. Slesinger and Richard L. Moyers, *A Snapshot of America's Nonprofit Boards: Results of a National Survey* (Washington, D.C.: National Center for Nonprofit Boards, 1995), 9. Used with permission.

Planning involves identifying the participants in and leaders of the diversity initiative. This can be accomplished through the establishment of a task force or special advisory committee, the use of consultants, or both. An assessment of board members' present attitudes and perceptions regarding diversity is a critical part of this first phase. An analysis of the composition of the board and its needs and roles in decision making, and a framework for a plan, also should emerge.

The second phase, building awareness, includes a variety of activities, such as informational meetings, sensitivity training, and development of a plan. The third phase, taking action, applies the plan to critical board development practices such as recruitment, orientation, and retention of members. It is in this phase that a board's commitment to inclusiveness is likely to be tested. Last in the process is the evaluation phase. This is an opportunity to step back and revisit the process, to learn what activities did or did not work well, and to make adjustments.

From six years of experience in multicultural organizational change, four Canadian United Way organizations have learned that success in achieving diversity initiatives is predicated on several factors:

- commitment emanating from the top of the organization
- clear identification of the necessary changes
- management of the process from within the organization
- the use of training to support the process
- informed decision making
- reflection of the change(s) in organizational policies and procedures
- action-oriented, measurable goals
- effective use of resources
- consideration of accountability.[13]

The experiences of these United Way organizations were part of a Canadian national project to (1) strengthen the nonprofit sector's capacity to provide culturally sensitive services and (2) enhance accessibility to services in an increasingly diverse society. The United Way of the Lower Mainland (British Columbia) designed a "Letter of Agreement" for its member agencies that participated in this multicultural development project. The letter not only describes the principles, conditions, and expected outcomes for participants in the project, but also asks for each agency's commitment to change. (A copy of this Letter of Agreement appears in Appendix D.) Such a document is a useful starting point in the development of a plan of action.

Creating a more accessible and inclusive organization requires building a diverse board. It can be a difficult process, as people are generally resistant to change, especially when the results are not immediately apparent. Nonetheless, the vitality of an organization is closely linked to effective management of diversity.

SUPPORTIVE STRUCTURES

A nonprofit's board of directors is legally responsible for its organization and for overseeing the chief executive. With the exception of organizations with voting memberships and those without paid staff, all nonprofit boards have these two roles in common. However, most boards take on broader responsibilities, and some create separate organizational structures to help distribute these duties. Larger complex organizations are more likely to create separate structures than smaller organizations.

Advisory Bodies

One of the most common supportive structures is an advisory body, sometimes called an advisory board. The word "board" in this context is actually a misnomer, as advisory bodies do not resemble governing boards in either responsibilities or authority. The term board should be applied only to an organization's governing body; advisory bodies may be called advisory councils or committees.

As its name implies, an advisory body is *advisory;* it has no real authority. It is a group of individuals assembled for some special purpose that meets less frequently than the board of directors, or only under special circumstances. An advisory body may conduct studies or make recommendations at the request of the board, the chief executive, or other department heads. It may be called on for advice in problem solving or planning. A nonprofit's chief executive is not accountable to an advisory body or obligated to heed its recommendations.

Advisory bodies are commonly used in direct or indirect fund-raising. For example, an organization may create a business advisory board composed of corporate executives. Busy executives sometimes prefer to play the role of an adviser rather than a board member because an advisory role presumably will take less of their time. A nonprofit's staff and board may use its business advisers to access major gift prospects. Sometimes prominent individuals, such as actors or athletic stars, lend their names to an advisory body on the assumption that prestigious names will attract attention to the organization and boost its prospects for raising money. These are examples of indirect fund-raising.

The National Advisory Council of the University of Utah is an example of an advisory body providing direct assistance in fund-raising. The Council's bylaws state that its fiduciary responsibilities are "to aid the University in connection with its financial and fiscal matters and needs, such as rendering assistance in obtaining funds and gifts from the private sector, including individuals, business organizations and foundations; and by way of specification but not in limitation, to assist and support the University of Utah's Permanent Endowment Fund." [14] The University uses the Council as a vehicle to bring alumni and other prominent people to campus twice a year for two-day meetings where department heads present reports of new programs requiring financial support. Council advisers are thoroughly updated on the University's activities and enjoy a round of social events during their campus visits. In their own communities, advisers act as ambassadors of good will for the University. Council members also have taken the initiative of contacting the University with development ideas and suggestions of prospective donors. This kind of exchange between an institution and its advisers occurs because a deliberate effort is made to use this group of individuals efficiently and effectively.

Specialized program support is another common use of advisory bodies. Seattle University's Institute of Public Service has created an advisory board that is separate from the University's Board of Trustees. The eighteen-member group is composed primarily of representatives from public service organizations (government and nonprofit agencies), and includes graduates of the program as well as two graduate student representatives. The advisory board does not meet on a regular basis; it is called together as needed, about once per quarter. The members contribute ideas to the faculty on the curriculum and marketing of the institute's Master of Public Administration program. The advisory board is an important link to the community because, collectively, the members have the knowledge and experience to make recommendations about what students need to know (e.g., skills and competencies) in order to become effective managers and leaders.

Unless there is a written document defining an advisory body's purpose and objectives, it is easy to lose sight of why it was created. It is important to periodically examine the activities of an advisory body and evaluate its usefulness. This can be relatively easy if the advisory body has a written work plan describing what it intends to accomplish in a given period of time (e.g., twelve to eighteen months). Such a mandate should originate from the board, but the group should be free to determine how it will implement board directives. In other instances, if an organization finds that it does not use the resources of its advisory body, or if the group does not enhance the work of the board but instead creates more work, the body should be disbanded.

An advisory body must be an integral part of the organization. The effectiveness and potential of any group is diminished if it exists outside an organization's framework. While the aforementioned Advisory Board of the Institute of Public Service at Seattle University is dedicated to the public administration program and its concerns are not by definition institution wide, it does not operate outside the purview of the university. Its mission statement reflects the University's mission.

One way to ensure that an advisory body functions within an organization's framework is to assign at least one member from the governing board or staff to serve as an ex-officio member of the group and attend its meetings. The ex-officio member reports to the executive and/or the board of directors on the advisers' activities, acts as a resource person, and helps keep the advisory group operating within the scope of the organization's mission by raising questions of relevance. Without some process for integrating an advisory body with the rest of the organization, the advisers, board members, or both groups may experience discomfort in the ambiguity of their respective roles. The following organization's experience illustrates the result of overlooking this potential problem.

A small-town community center's board of directors formed a task force of community representatives to create a long-range plan for the center. In the board's eagerness to let the task force operate without interference, they did not assign a liaison to the committee. This oversight created a dilemma regarding ownership. The task force was charged with creating a plan, but the board would eventually be responsible for overseeing its implementation. This raised several questions in the minds of board members.

- Was the board of directors willing to approve and commit to a plan created by another group?
- What if the board or center staff disagreed with segments of the plan and elected not to implement it?

- How might the board's response to the committee's recommendations impact the organization's future efforts to involve community residents in some planning endeavor?

It was important that both the board of directors and the citizens task force feel ownership for the end product, the long-range plan. There are several options this board could have adopted to assure dual ownership of the center's plan.

- A board member could attend all the task force meetings and report back to the board.
- Rotation of board liaisons could avoid overburdening already busy board members.
- The liaison could act as a resource person, an observer, a reporter, or some combination.
- The task force could arrange for one or two joint meetings with the board of directors when decisions regarding the plan's content and action strategies needed to be made.

Four months into the planning process, the community center's board did opt to use a rotating liaison to report on the committee's activities at board meetings. By introducing a means for these two bodies to interact, the board alleviated the uncertainty the task force felt regarding its role and its relationship with the board of directors, and the board's own concern about dominating the planning process was mitigated.

In summary, if advisory bodies or other supportive groups such as auxiliaries are important enough to be created to help an organization achieve its goals, then they deserve the same kind of cultivation and nurturing that a board of directors receives, as well as the freedom to pursue their assigned tasks.

Foundation Boards

Organizations sometimes create separate nonprofit corporations called foundations, not to be confused with private (grant-making) foundations. In addition to the responsibilities common to any nonprofit board, some institutions' boards (e.g., colleges and universities, hospitals, research centers) have unique technically oriented oversight responsibilities that call for people with specialized knowledge. Fund-raising expertise is not necessarily a quality of a board member with expert knowledge of a discipline and its practices. Establishment of a separate foundation and foundation board of directors satisfies an institution's need for a group of people with fund-raising experience and knowledge of investment management.

Other circumstances in which a foundation is useful include the following:

1. When an organization receives a substantial portion of its operating funds through government contracting or third-party reimbursements, a separate nonprofit foundation can be useful for attracting private sector dollars as well as keeping its public and private funds from intermingling.

2. Some organizations, by their mission or geographic location, are governed by a constituent, or neighborhood-based, board of directors. In this situation, the board may lack ties to the business community that are helpful in leveraging private funding; a separate fund-raising board could provide that linkage.

Foundations are not a good idea for every organization, because additional time and energy on the part of staff and the board is required to establish and manage a foundation. An organization needs to determine whether a foundation will really make a difference in achieving its mission. For example, a fear of fund-raising or reluctance to ask for money is not uncommon among nonprofit boards but is not a good reason for creating a foundation.

A colleague observed a social services agency spend two years trying to put together a foundation board to raise money: "At the end [of the two years] they had failed, they wasted all that time and energy. That same energy could have been put towards asking for money rather than asking others to ask for them." [15] This raises the question of why an individual would want to raise money for an organization but have no voice in its governance. The dedicated individuals already on a board of directors are a nonprofit's best advocates; given their strong belief in their organization, these members are usually in the best position to successfully sell its cause.

Voting Memberships

In its articles of incorporation and bylaws, a nonprofit may identify some body beyond the board of directors with ultimate authority for the organization, typically called a voting membership. This organizational model is found primarily among associations and fraternal and federated organizations. For example, the voting membership of the National Mental Health Association is composed of delegates from mental health associations from various states. Members meet once a year and are empowered to vote on policy issues such as standards of affiliation, bylaw changes, program initiatives, and fiscal practices. The voting membership provides guidance to the board of directors.

The Shriners, a well-known fraternal organization with a highly complex structure, provides a classic example of a voting membership:

> The 191 Shrine Temples are governed by the Imperial Council, which is composed of Representatives. The Representatives of the Imperial Council include all past and present Imperial Officers; Emeritus Representatives (those who have served 15 years or more); and Representatives elected from each Temple. . . . These Representatives meet once a year . . . to make policy decisions and legislation regarding both the fraternity and the hospitals. With nearly 900 Representatives, the Imperial Council constitutes once of the largest legislative bodies in the world. The Representatives also elect the Imperial Officers and the chairman and members of the Board of Trustees for Shriners Hospitals for Crippled Children.[16]

Voting memberships rarely meet more than once a year. At the annual meeting, members may elect the board of directors and officers, approve long-range plans, propose or vote on changes to the bylaws, discuss and take action on other issues related to significant changes in the association, and resolve other matters as prescribed in the nonprofit's bylaws. Between annual membership meetings, the board acts like an executive committee for the full membership and conducts itself like other nonprofit boards.

CHANGING STRUCTURE TO MEET CHANGING NEEDS: A CASE STUDY

The Hospice of the Florida Suncoast is an example of an organization with an extended board structure. As this organization has grown, so has its need for some very specific linkages with its large geographic service area. Its response has been to spin off separate 501(c)(3) organizations, each with its own governing board. The integrity of the three Hospice boards can be attributed to strong leadership, clearly defined board roles and responsibilities, and a systematic approach to organizing board work. Maintaining this complex structure is made easier by the organization's large staff, which is assisted by a core of committed program volunteers.

The Hospice of the Florida Suncoast, in Largo, Florida, was founded in 1977 by a group of volunteers who were concerned about the special needs of terminally ill people and their families. Over the years, this organization has grown to be the largest nonprofit community-based hospice in the nation. The Hospice's organizational chart in Exhibit 3.3 shows the organization's various administrative and program areas and illustrates the complexity of this nonprofit.

The Hospice serves more than 1,200 patients each day; employs 750 people, of whom 600 are full-time professional health-care workers; has an annual budget of $54 million; and uses more than 2,000 volunteers, who provide approximately 70,000 volunteer hours each year. To serve the terminally ill and provide support to their families, the Hospice operates two hospice houses, provides care and support to more than 300 patients in one hundred area nursing homes, and provides care to approximately 900 patients in their own homes. Because of the international reputation this organization has earned, the Hospice of the Florida Suncoast is frequently called upon to consult with other hospices.

The Hospice is a complex corporation that includes three separate 501(c)(3) organizations with different missions, but the same goals. Each has its own board of directors: the Hospice Board of Directors ("Care Board"), the Foundation Board of Trustees, and the Hospice Institute Board of Directors. The Care Board is the original board of directors established at the organization's founding. This sixteen-member board oversees program operations, planning, and special projects of the Hospice program. The function of the board, as stated in its written roles and responsibilities, is to establish and develop policy as a guide in planning activities and programs. The administrator implements the policy with staff, and develops procedures and activities to meet organizational goals. Board responsibilities can include legal, fiduciary, and management components.[17] The Care Board has five standing committees: Executive Committee, Committee on Directors, Bylaws Committee, Strategic Quality Committee, and Community Outreach/Public Policy Committee. The Strategic Quality Committee oversees the work of several advisory committees: Managed Care, Ethics, Clergy Council, Nursing Home, Inpatient Residential, and Children's Support. The Community Outreach/Public Policy Committee also oversees the work of several advisory committees: Public Relations, Community Out-

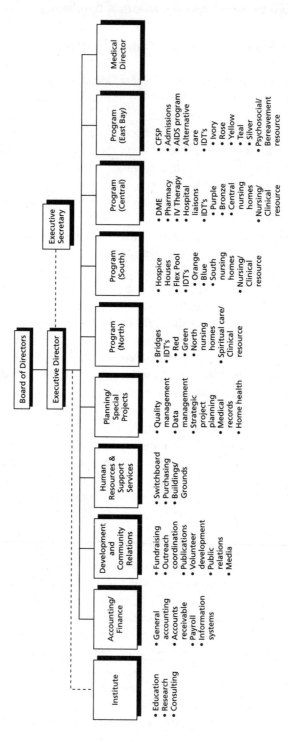

Exhibit 3.3 The Hospice of the Florida Suncoast: Hospice Home Health Agency

Source: The Hospice of the Florida Suncoast. Reprinted with permission.

reach, Jewish Hospice, and Asian Outreach. The chief executive is the key staffperson on the Care Board, but other managers staff the various committees. Exhibit 3.4 gives an overview of the organization of the Care Board.

The twenty-three-member Hospice Foundation Board of Trustees was originally established to support the Care Board in its fund-raising responsibilities; in addition, it now supports the Hospice Institute. As depicted in Exhibit 3.5, it has five standing committees (Executive, Major Gifts, Finance/Investment, Parliamentary, Special Events) and four ad hoc committees. The Parliamentary Committee, consisting of an attorney and an expert on *Robert's Rules of Order*, acts as gatekeeper for the board; its task is to assure that corporate decisions are consistent with the bylaws and articles of incorporation. The director of development and community relations serves as the key staff member on Foundation Board.

The Hospice Institute was recently established as a separate 501(c)(3) organization. The corporation needed to ensure there would be no comingling of funds for research and education programs and for the hospice's patient-care programs, especially since patient programs receive Medicare reimbursements. The new institute also provides donors with clear lines of distinction between its research and education activities and the patient-care programs of the hospice.

The Hospice Institute's board has sixteen members; its bylaws identify six committees (Operations, Executive, Finance, Trustees, Parliamentary, Development/Community Relations) and define their roles. The Operations Committee is divided into three subgroups—education, research, consulting—that oversee those respective areas of the Institute's program. The Trustees Committee acts as the nominating committee, is responsible for analyzing the strengths and weaknesses of the board, and takes responsibility for board members' orientation. The Development/Community Relations Committee oversees matters pertaining to community relations and community development; it also is involved in fund-raising in cooperation with the Foundation Board, but fund-raising is not this committee's main focus. Each committee includes at least three Institute members (who serve on more than one board committee), as well as representatives from the community. The Institute's director serves as key staffperson on the board; the board does not have hiring or firing authority over the Institute Director, because she is accountable to the chief executive.

All three boards are involved in strategic planning; the results of their individual planning efforts are shared, and they collaborate on setting priorities for the entire hospice corporation. The chair of each board is an ex-

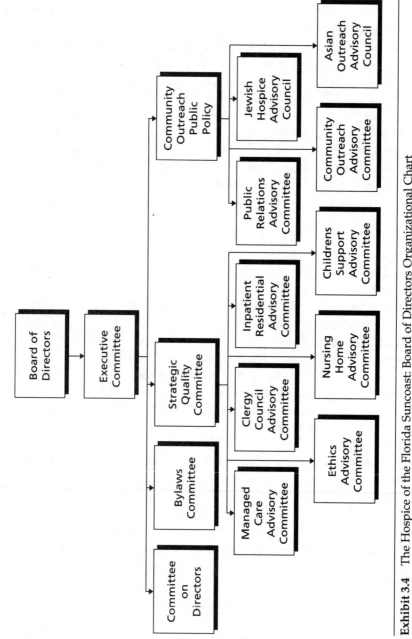

Exhibit 3.4 The Hospice of the Florida Suncoast: Board of Directors Organizational Chart

Source: The Hospice of the Florida Suncoast. Reprinted with permission.

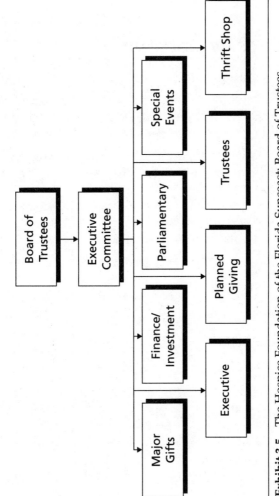

Exhibit 3.5   The Hospice Foundation of the Florida Suncoast: Board of Trustees Organizational Chart

Source: The Hospice of the Florida Suncoast. Reprinted with permission.

officio member of the other two boards. A joint meeting of all three boards is held annually.

Rather than becoming overwhelmed by the challenge of implementing new health care directives, the chief executive of the Hospice Institute reports that major changes affecting the health-care field have served only to heighten board members' interest: "It seems the more they get involved, the more they want to be involved." [18]

SUGGESTIONS FOR FURTHER READING

United Way of Greater Metropolitan Toronto. "Action, Access, Diversity: A Guide to Multicultural/Anti-Racist Organizational Change for Social Service Agencies." 1991. Report available through the United Way at: 26 Wellington St., E., 11th floor, Toronto, Ontario M5E 1W9, Canada.

Widmer, Candice. "Minority Participation of Boards of Directors of Human Services: Some Evidence and Suggestions." *Journal of Voluntary Action Research* (March 1988).

CHAPTER FOUR

Organizing the Board's Work

M any nonprofit executives have said that all that is needed to get something done is a board of directors with the right mix of people. The people associated with an organization certainly do make a difference, but a good operating structure that clearly defines roles, expectations, functions, and processes will help any board of directors conduct its business more efficiently. Even those individuals with prior nonprofit board experience require orientation and training, because every organization has a different way of operating. One of the things a board member should learn during orientation is how the board organizes its work and delegates authority.

This chapter discusses (1) the working structures of a board, such as committees; (2) alternatives for organizing the board's work; (3) board development as a strategy to help members learn their roles and responsibilities; and (4) board development as an opportunity for self-renewal.

WORKING STRUCTURES

Aside from legal obligations, the responsibilities of a board of directors vary, but generally can be divided into seven broad categories:

- clarification of the organization's mission
- interpretation of the mission to the public
- establishment of goals, long-range plans, and strategic plans
- setting policies and other major guidelines for operation

- protecting the organization's financial stability and solvency
- hiring, supporting, and assessing the performance of the executive director
- evaluation of the performance of the organization and of the board itself.

In addition to understanding and accepting these responsibilities, a board must create an operational structure for conducting its business efficiently. Committees are one means to that end.

Not all boards have a committee structure. Some are too small to be subdivided. Others prefer to form task forces as needed. Still others prefer to behave as a committee of the whole. However, most nonprofit boards do use committees; basic committee structures should be outlined in an organization's bylaws. Often there is a bylaw empowering the chairperson to name committees as needed, thereby enabling the board to adapt to the changing needs of the organization.

The Role of Committees

Board committees should be formed to help the board of directors conduct its business rather than to augment the functions of the organization's staff. Committees are vehicles for parceling out the board's work and removing more mundane tasks from the full board's consideration. For example, policy issues should be deliberated at the full-board level, whereas the details of the purchase of a new facility are best hammered out at the committee level.

The use of committees to accomplish certain tasks is based on the premise that smaller groups can conduct themselves more efficiently than the whole. A well-defined committee structure is required for efficient operation. Committees offer individuals an opportunity to contribute specific talents and expertise, or to follow their special interests. Committees also serve as training grounds for board members to take on positions of increasing responsibility, such as board officer. The committee structure encourages broader participation on the part of board members.

Some committees also have an advisory function. They meet separately from the full board to discuss agenda items assigned by the board chairperson, the full board, or a committee chairperson. They report to the full board with their findings and recommend action to be taken. In this capacity committees may *initiate* policy. However, there is a distinction between committees advising the board of directors as a whole and committees usurping the full board's power or authority. If a board adopts committee recommendations without question or discussion and simply rubber-stamps its work, members' effective participation is reduced.[1] Committees must not lose sight of the fact that the full board is the definitive body of the organization.

Board committees may fulfill one of four general purposes, being oriented to administration, liaison work, study, or projects.[2] Administrative committees deal with the managerial issues of the organization. (This refers to oversight, not involvement in operations.) A liaison committee promotes communication among the organization, its stakeholders, the media, and other community groups. Study committees focus on new directions or emerging issues. Project committees pick up where study committees leave off by planning or monitoring new programs.

The above types of committees may be either standing or ad hoc. *Standing committees* are permanent committees identified in an organization's bylaws. They are expected to meet regularly and conduct activities that will lead to the accomplishment of a set of prescribed objectives. Standing committees are discussed in more detail later in this chapter.

Ad hoc committees are established for a specific purpose and disbanded when their jobs are done; they are not described in the bylaws. For example, study committees are often ad hoc because they are formed to review and generate recommendations on a specific issue. Ad hoc committees should not supplant the work of the board's standing committees. When a special issue or new business arises, the board chairperson should consider the capacity of an existing, standing committee to handle the matter before undertaking the formation of another committee.

Types of Board Committees

A 1995 survey by the National Center for Nonprofit Boards (NCNB) found that nonprofit boards have an average of 6.6 standing committees. The types most frequently cited were executive, finance/budget, and nominating (in that order), followed by development/fund-raising, program, and long-range planning. The least frequently cited types of standing committees were public relations and audit, respectively.[3]

It is interesting to note that "personnel committee" was not among the choices of committees on the questionnaire; and, according to the published findings, it was not cited as an "other committee" by respondents. This represents a significant change in thinking about the roles of boards and their committees. A standing personnel board committee is no longer considered appropriate, because its existence provides a temptation to micromanage. After personnel policies are in place, there is nothing for this type of committee to do but get inappropriately involved in personnel affairs.[4] It is the executive's job (or the personnel manager in larger organizations) to maintain a working environment conducive to attracting and keeping quality personnel, to assure compliance with the Equal Employment Opportunity Commission (EEOC), and to assess and plan for future personnel requirements, among other things. A board's involvement in personnel matters should be limited to oversight of the executive's performance and any major personnel policy revisions. The latter can be carried out by a board task force.

Traditional Board Committees and their Functions

Executive Committee.   With few exceptions, nonprofit boards are authorized in organization bylaws to form executive committees that can function on behalf of full boards in emergencies or interim situations. Bylaws should limit the power of an executive committee by stating that its authority can not circumvent the responsibility and authority placed in the full board of directors. This committee is powerful by definition and poses a danger if it usurps the full board. It should not function as a decision-making body between board meetings except in organizations with large national boards or voting memberships (see Chapter 3) that meet only once a year.

Most organizations rely on their executive committees to make better use of the full board's time. For example, executive committees are used to review or prepare board meeting agendas to ensure that all matters coming before the board are relevant and appropriate, or they may plan the board's work and make committee assignments.

The executive committee is typically composed of the officers of the board and may include the chairpersons of standing committees. It is wise to balance the executive committee with a few other board members or select committee representatives other than committee chairpersons, as committee chairs are appointed by the board chairperson and thus may be biased toward a single point of view. Past board officers may be included on this committee; the organization's executive is an ex-officio member. The executive committee should represent the board's leadership because, as previously stated, it has the authority to act in crisis and interim situations.

Finance Committee.   The finance committee's chief responsibility is to recommend policy regarding the agency's finances and assets; this includes setting limits on the executive's power to incur debt or dispense funds without board approval. This committee might also provide an oversight function for those boards assuming responsibility for safeguarding endowment or reserve funds.[5] A finance committee should not become involved in budgeting, which is primarily a staff responsibility. The review of an organization's financial statements is better attended to by the full board rather than a few committee members, because all board members carry a fiduciary responsibility for the nonprofit.

In a very small organization, the finance committee, or board treasurer, may actually prepare financial reports, approve payment of bills, perform other bookkeeping functions, and advise the board when income and expenditures are out of balance. Nonprofit organizations should have an annual audit conducted by a certified public accountant. When an executive does not feel qualified to hire an auditor and supervise the audit process, the finance committee may fulfill that function.

Resource Development Committee. A resource development, or fund-raising, committee is always a standing committee, except in organizations that do not need to raise funds. Some organizations earn their annual income from service fees or other income-producing activities. In those rare cases, a resource development committee would be assembled only if a special program or capital project required new or supplemental funding. While the entire board of directors is responsible for the organization's solvency, the resource development committee ensures that funds are raised to enable the organization to conduct its business. The broader term *development* encourages consideration of ways to finance an organization beyond charitable solicitations (e.g., earned income, fees, contracting). And, the term *resource* encompasses more than cash donations. Organizations also need goods and equipment, donated services, and so forth.

A philosophy of fund development is essential to the work of the resource development committee. Such a philosophy takes into account preferences regarding sources of funds (e.g., private funds versus government funds); methods of fund-raising (e.g., the appropriateness of gambling ventures such as bingo); and values and attitudes regarding fund-raising. These various elements should be discussed in relation to the organization's overall capacity for raising funds and its budgetary needs; the committee should then recommend the resulting set of funding principles to the board to guide its fund-raising endeavors. (See Chapter 5 for further discussion of a board's fund-raising responsibilities.)

Nominating Committee. This standing committee, responsible for the nomination and development of new board members, is often used in a manner that limits its potential. Too often a nominating committee meets one month before the board's annual meeting and hurriedly prepares a slate of nominees. When inadequate attention is given to the selection of new board members, inappropriate board membership may result. Instead, the nominating committee should be responsible for maintaining an updated file of prospective board members, enabling it to bring a list of carefully selected nominees to the board whenever a vacancy occurs.

There is a trend toward enlarging this committee's responsibilities to include some of the following functions:

- orientation of new board members
- planning of annual board retreats or other board educational events
- supervision of the board's training activities
- alerting board members to other volunteer training opportunities in the community
- assessment the board's performance.

Adopting the name "development committee" reminds board members that this committee has broader areas of responsibility than the nomination of prospective members. (Board development is further discussed later in this chapter.)

Community and Public Relations Committee.   Each board member is an emissary for the organization and should take advantage of opportunities to interpret the organization's mission to the public. However, a community and public relations committee oversees the organization's interaction with other community groups and in general ensures that the organization assumes a coordinated approach to the resolution of community problems. Depending on the size of a nonprofit and the nature of its services, a board's community and public relations committee would either recommend explicit policies or assume direct responsibility for the following areas:

- access to other agencies in the community
- communications' techniques
- planning collaborative activities with other community groups
- monitoring the organization's representation at major community events or public hearings.

A large organization with a professional marketing or public relations staff does not need the board to be involved with public relations other than setting policy regarding the above areas. A small organization without such staff needs additional help from the board's community and public relations committee to set public relations goals, identify stakeholders for targeted messages, direct demographic research on the organization's constituency, access the media, and advise on contracting with advertising and public relations counsel for major events and special campaigns. This committee should review and evaluate the impact of the organization's publicity, be alert to organizational problems that may require sensitive interpretation, and generally work to ensure that the organization enjoys a good public image.

Program Committee. The functions of a board program committee are to:

- prepare policy recommendations pertaining to program direction
- evaluate how the organization can best serve the community in a changing, turbulent environment
- study the ramifications of program expansion or contraction
- oversee program accountability
- monitor organization and program evaluations
- assure that the organization is making progress toward fulfilling its mission and goals and providing quality services.

If a board of directors functions as a policy-centered board according to Carver's governance model (see Chapter 1), it will not have a program committee because program is clearly a staff responsibility. As with a personnel committee, the existence of a program committee provides a risk of overinvolvement, a temptation for board members to implement program rather than focus on policy. However, NCNB's survey showed that 47 percent of the respondents had standing board program committees.

An Alternative Way to Organize Board Work

When a nonprofit organization's bylaws identify standing board committees, the board of directors forms these committees in order to comply with the rules of operation, regardless of whether or not they are really needed. As a result, a board starts out by thinking of itself in terms of its parts. Carver's governance-theory model offers an alternative viewpoint that emphasizes *board holism.* The integrity of the board's wholeness becomes the primary consideration in how a board of directors conducts its business; the practice of dividing labor through committees is the antithesis. This approach is guided by the principle of minimalism. Abiding by this principle preserves the integrity of the board as a governing body and the separateness of the executive's role, and it serves to protect the board-executive accountability relationship.[6] The appropriate path, according to this theory, is to begin with *no* committees and add them only as necessary. This would require a change in the bylaws of most nonprofit organizations; sections that specify committees by name must be struck. A general clause calling for all committees to be formed on an as-needed basis then should be inserted to give maximum flexibility in board operating structure.

According to the Carver model, a board can create unified policies only by acting as a whole. Thus a primary responsibility of committees is to help the full board of directors in its decision making. Theoretically, the best decisions are ones that result from (1) carefully examining all possible choices, (2) weighing the consequences of the various alternatives, and (3) deciding on an optimal course of action. The function of board committees is to review policy alternatives and their consequences before issues are brought to the full board for a vote. This enables the board to make informed decisions and concentrate on the selection of a course of action.

The types of committees that might be formed by a board operating under the Carver model of governance reflect four broad areas of policy rather than areas of administration: (1) ends (goals), (2) executive limitations, (3) board process, and (4) board-executive relationship.[7]

Ultimately, a board's committee structure should mirror the needs of the nonprofit organization. The key variable in the role and function of board committees (and the board itself) is the presence or absence of full-time professional staff.[8] A policy-focused governing board along the lines of Carver's model is undoubtedly appropriate for many nonprofit organizations, but it is not every organization's ideal. Some nonprofits still need their boards of directors to help fill management voids.

Rules for Effective Committees

Any committee structure can be effective when the following elements are present:

1. All committees have specific tasks and a clear direction. Committee members know the limits of their authority but also appreciate their potential.

2. Committee chairpersons are capable of facilitating decision-making processes.

3. When a committee includes program staff, care is taken to utilize that resource. The committee maintains control of its own work and does not defer judgment to the organization's staff.

4. Committee members are willing to give whatever time is required to their fact-finding, evaluation, or other activities. Assignments are short-term to maintain interest and motivation.

5. Good working relationships are established and maintained within the committee itself and with other members of the board.

6. The committee chairperson ensures that the committee does not work in isolation, but is an integral subsystem of the whole organization.

7. Committees conduct their business in a timely fashion.

The last point is more significant than it may appear. A decision or recommendation stalled in committee can cause delays in an important timetable for the organization.

BOARD DEVELOPMENT

The Benefits of an Educated Board

Nonprofit boards of directors can impact an entire community because they set policy for agencies that provide health, education, welfare, recreation, cultural, or other services. Membership on a nonprofit board is more than a position of honor: "It is a profound community trust [and] effective participation on the board is something which can and may be learned." [9] The education of board members should be ongoing for several reasons:

1. Nonprofit organizations are complex and changing; boards need to adapt to new technologies, new methods of operation, and new developments in their fields.

2. The role of nonprofit board members is changing along with that of the organizations they serve.

3. There are new approaches to effective nonprofit leadership and governance.[10]

While boards generally expect their organizations' staffs to be professionally trained, it is important to recognize that, through systematic training, board members can enhance their own leadership skills and competencies and increase their knowledge. This improvement in board members' skills results in an organization better able to serve its constituents and the community at large.

Orientation of New Members

The recruitment process is actually the initial stage of orientation. Prospective board members are introduced to the organization's mission, goals, and programs and to the role of the board of directors. Some organizations conduct orientation sessions for prospective members, others hold them for new members only once they have come on the board. The purpose of board orientation is to give new members information about the organization's operations and programs and clarifying information about their roles as board members.

A planned, systematic approach to orientation is best. The following outline suggests one approach that can be modified to suit different circumstances.

I. Plan the orientation program.
   A. During recruitment, prospects should have learned what is generally expected of them as members of the board of directors. The board's written job description should include a statement that participation in orientation is mandatory, so it will not come as a surprise when one or two days (not necessarily consecutive) are spent on orientation activities.
   B. Plan the distribution of materials in accordance with each orientation activity. Too much written material too soon is overwhelming. For example, it is not necessary to hand out program brochures and information on the clients served until the tour of the agency's facility.
   C. Use the background data gathered during recruitment to tailor presentations according to new members' personal and professional interests.
   D. Consider assigning a sponsor—a more experienced board member—to each new member; make sure the purpose of this relationship is clear to both parties.
II. Orient new members to the organization.
   A. Schedule a meeting with the chief executive. This conference gives the newcomer an opportunity to ask specific questions about the

organization's operations. For the executive, meeting with new board members provides a chance to establish a good working relationship early on.

B. Plan a tour of the agency. If the organization is a campus facility, visit one building of every type (e.g., a classroom building, a dormitory, a sports facility). Even if the organization is not facility-based, a visit to the office where the organization conducts its business is desirable. When an organization has several program sites in the community, all of them should be visited. Board members will be called upon to make decisions regarding the organization's physical plant, so on-site visits are important.

C. Prepare a brief two- or three-page synopsis of key organizational demographics: number of clients/students/patients, program milestones, major program changes over the past five to ten years, staff roster, trends, and other appropriate data to supplement oral presentations.

D. Arrange for new members to attend a staff meeting or briefing session by the staff. They should have the opportunity to meet other key personnel, learn about their respective areas of responsibility, and ask questions.

III. Orient members to the board.

A. Have the board chairperson make a welcoming call or visit to all new members.

B. Distribute a biographical sketch on the full board, including members' terms of office, offices held, committee assignments, places and positions of employment, addresses and phone numbers, and other relevant information.

C. Hold an informal social function to help integrate new members with the rest of the board.

D. Schedule a meeting for all new board members with the executive committee and other committee chairpersons. This gives newcomers a chance to become acquainted with the board's leadership and with the activities of the committees. A discussion of board procedures, directors' roles, responsibilities and liabilities, and major issues facing the organization provides new members with additional perspectives on the whole organization.

E. Distribute the board manual or workbook, which should include bylaws, policies, organizational charts, board committees, rosters of staff and board members and officers, and other pertinent information.

F. Provide time for a debriefing among the new members, board chairperson, and chief executive so any remaining questions and concerns can be clarified. Debriefing sessions also can be an opportunity to ask new board members which parts of the orientation were most helpful, which were the least helpful, and how future board orientations might be improved.

A thorough orientation is very important because it provides new board members with information critical to the fulfillment of their governance obligations. In some organizations, new members are not permitted to vote until they have completed their orientation. This type of mandate motivates new members to complete the orientation process as soon as possible, and enables them to make more informed decisions.

Training and Sustaining Board Members

New member orientation is only the first phase in the board's education and development. It is followed by systematic communications between the board and the organization's staff, regularly scheduled retreats or renewal sessions, and occasional training programs or workshops on special topics. (See discussion in Chapter 6 regarding effective communication.) A medium-sized or large board can charge its nominating/development committee with the responsibility for board education. A smaller board may elect to form an ad hoc committee to plan board educational activities as needed. Either type of planning group can more effectively fulfill its function by adhering to the following principles of board development:

- Carefully formulate a purpose for all board development activities.
- Set realistic training objectives.
- When planning an activity, consider the unique needs and interests of all members of the board.
- Consider different types of development activities, such as in-house training, guest speakers or consultants, and workshops or conferences.
- Evaluate each educational activity.

The full board should be involved in the selection of issues to be addressed in board development training; the committee should set specific training objectives, decide on appropriate content and formats, manage the logistics, and perform other related tasks. Approaching board development in this way increases the likelihood of full participation.

In addition to helping a board learn how to operate more effectively, a good program of board development sustains members' interest in the organization and in the board. When board members are well informed and trained to carry out a board's primary functions, they are more comfortable with, and are more likely to remain committed to, their roles.

The use of a development program by a nonprofit board sends a positive message to its members that the organization values their contributions enough to invest extra time and sometimes funds. Development programs give board members an opportunity for self-renewal and for quality time away from business as usual. In short, the ongoing education of a nonprofit board is an excellent strategy for nurturing and motivating board members.

SUGGESTIONS FOR FURTHER READING

Collard, Eileen, and Sandra Haff. "Relationships: The Key to Effective Committees." In *The Nonprofit Board Book,* Anthes et al., eds. Hampton: Independent Community Consultants, 1985.

Fram, Eugene H., and Robert F. Pearse. *The High-Performance Nonprofit: A Management Guide for Boards and Executives.* Milwaukee: Families International, 1992.

Nonprofit Committees Series, four booklets on different types of board committees, available through the National Center for Nonprofit Boards: 2000 L St., NW, #510-T; Washington, D.C., 20036-4907; 202/452-6262.

CHAPTER FIVE

The Core Responsibilities of a Nonprofit Board

An organization is guided and defined by its plans and policies. This chapter emphasizes the importance of setting clear policies and planning strategically. A nonprofit board's role in the critical areas of policy, planning, fiscal control, and fund-raising are discussed, with examples of how the boards of various organizations have approached these core responsibilities successfully.

POLICIES AND PLANS

The Nature of Policy

A survey of corporations conducted by the Conference Board resulted in several definitions of the term *policy:* "A broad interest, direction, or philosophy; an expression of the corporation's principles and objectives; guides to thinking and action; general standards not subject to frequent change; and procedures and practices." [1] These different interpretations show that it can be difficult to distinguish policy setting from other elements of planning or differentiate between levels of policies. Generally, a policy has the following characteristics:

- focus on critical issues
- guide to action
- broad statement of intent
- expression of values or perspectives
- presentation of the philosophy of an organization

69

- establishment of limits
- resolution of questions about how an organization generally conducts its business in the present and future
- long-term applicability at the higher levels of an organization's operations
- inclusion of different levels of operation.

An organization may have a policy without a plan to implement it, or vice versa. There may be a policy stating that the organization vigorously supports a program of staff development, but the organization may not yet have planned such training. Alternatively, an organization's five-year plan may include annual training programs or other staff development activities without such a policy statement. The existence of a major policy can force formation of a plan. Policies can be either guides to planning or derivatives of planning.

Policies are commonly grouped into six levels: major, secondary, functional, minor, standard operating procedures and rules.[2]

- *Major policies* cover fundamental issues pertaining to mission, code of ethics, values and priorities, or other guiding principles of the organization.
- *Secondary policies* address questions about who the organization serves, the organization's geographic service areas, program priorities, and organizational resources (e.g., personnel, facilities, finances).
- *Functional policies* address general management areas such as administration, budgeting, planning, and marketing.
- *Minor policies* govern routine practices (e.g., membership, special projects, maintenance, employee contributions, advertising).
- *Standard operating procedures* outline the handling of various types of transactions such as travel reimbursements, maintenance records, requisitions, and registration of complaints. These lower-level policies are *process oriented*—they define how to do something.
- *Rules of conduct* consist of organizational norms that have been institutionalized (e.g., a dress code), or rules pertaining to employees' behavior (e.g., policies regarding smoking on premises and substance abuse).

The combination of different levels of policy constitutes the *policy structure* of an organization. While Exhibit 5.1 gives examples of the issues per-

Policy Level	Issue
Major	Merger with another organization
	Expansion of program into new area
Secondary	Establishment of an outreach program
	Major equipment or facility acquisition
	Basis for compensation (e.g., performance-based, equity-based, tenure-driven)
Functional	Budgeting process
	Fee schedule
	Criteria for personnel evaluation
	Collaborative purchasing (e.g., bulk purchases through a cooperative)
Minor	Participation in a united funds campaign
	Selection of contract services
Standard Operating Procedures	Payroll distribution
Rules	Requests for leave of absence
	Parking
	Smoking on premises
	Dress code

Exhibit 5.1 Issues Occurring at Different Policy Levels

taining to the six policy levels, in practice policy decisions do not fall neatly into hierarchical categories; they often may overlap, and a given organization does not necessarily have six levels or categories of policy.

Setting Policy

Understanding the nature and purpose of policy is the first step in policy development. The staff is best qualified to identify the organization's specific policy needs because they have the most intimate knowledge of the organization. It is the executive's responsibility to assess those needs and determine if they (1) might be addressed under an existing lower-level policy, (2) require new procedures or rules that can be set by management, or (3) deal with issues that should be brought before the board of directors.

There is little disagreement that setting policy is a primary role of a non-profit board of directors. The board is responsible for deciding which policy levels require its involvement. Some boards elect to establish only major policies; others may set policies at the major and secondary levels. Those with no staff are engaged by necessity in policy setting at all levels. The organization's manual of operations or board manual should describe clearly those policies that are within the board's purview and those that belong to the management staff.

There are four general steps to policy-setting at any level. The first is to define the policy objective(s) or purpose. Why is a policy needed? What will be accomplished by a policy statement on a particular issue? Policies should be based on facts rather than opinion. When a new policy is under consideration, an organization's executive should take a leadership role in informing the board of the issues at stake and the context from which the policy emerged.

The second step is to prepare a policy statement with the following characteristics:[3]

- *Explicit.* It is obvious that policies should be in writing. Statements such as, "We all know that," or, "that's understood," often crop up in discussions about policy. In putting what is thought to be generally understood in writing, and attempting to reach a consensus on the language of the policy statement, a board may find that there is far less agreement than was previously believed.

- *Current.* Outdated policies have no value. A board of directors may never quite get around to policy review until a crisis forces an examination of existing policies. To help ensure that policies are kept current, a board might preface its discussion of a particular issue by referring to the organization's policy manual.

- *Literal.* Policies must clearly state their meaning. Anyone reading a policy statement should know exactly what it means without having to make assumptions about its context or purpose.

- *Centrally located.* All policies should be kept in one manual. Board and staff should have equal access to the organization's policy manual.

- *Concise.* The longer a policy statement, the greater the chance for its meaning to become obscured. For example, it is not necessary to devote five pages to a policy of facility usage. And, the greater the number of policies, the harder it is to get a clear picture of the organization's operations.

Depending on their respective levels of experience in framing policy statements, either the board or the administrative staff may do the actual writing.

The third stage in policy-setting is implementation, which usually does not involve the board of directors unless the organization does not have the staff expertise to implement a particular policy. In such a case, the board chairperson might ask one or two trustees to manage whatever tasks are involved in implementation. For example, the board may establish a functional-level policy regarding investments and assign an investment banker and a certified public accountant from the board to help staff set up appropriate investment accounts. Another exception is an organization that is experiencing some kind of difficulty. The board may find it necessary to closely monitor how a policy is carried out by conducting on-site checks. Whatever the situation, a board should become involved in implementing policy only for a specific purpose and for a limited time.

The final stage of policy-setting is evaluation. Policies are established and implemented but too often never revisited to determine if they have had the desired effect. An organization's executive is responsible for informing the board about the intended and unintended consequences of higher-level policies as well as the impact of lower-level policies on the organization's operations. The board is responsible for asking questions to determine whether or not policies are producing the desired results.

Without policy directives, an organization may find that its operations flounder in inconsistency. It is a board's responsibility to ensure that policy statements are thoughtfully derived and consistent with the organization's mission.

Long-Range and Strategic Planning

Planning is the rational and systematic determination of where an organization presently stands, where it hopes to be, and how it will get there. It is a process concerned with the future impact of decisions that are made in the present.[4] Goals and objectives are set and resources are allocated to support activities that will take an organization where it wants to go.

All organizations should be involved in planning, but any of the following circumstances can trigger the need for additional planning or a review of existing plans:

1. organizational growth
2. unstable funding
3. demand for expanded services
4. expansion of an organization's role(s)

5. accountability to an oversight body

6. leadership changes

7. legislative mandates

8. desire to integrate departments or change the organization's structure

9. desire to change direction or vision

10. change in political climate.[5]

The complexity of organizational life pushes most organizations into creating several types of plans—long range, strategic, operational, capital, program, and others. Long-range and strategic plans encompass the entire organization as opposed to one area of operation, and focus on the organization's most pressing concerns.

Some management theorists make no distinction between long-range and strategic planning. However, while both types of planning may ultimately achieve similar outcomes, there are fundamental differences between the two in the way planning is approached and in the types of questions that are addressed. The features of long-range planning and strategic planning are compared in Exhibit 5.2.

Long-Range Planning	*Strategic Planning*
• General and inclusive; all aspects of the organization's mission are addressed	• Specifically focused on critical issues or prioritized goals
• Oriented toward identifying goals, objectives, and essential resources	• Oriented toward action; based on a range of possible futures
• Starts from the assumption the environment will remain relatively constant	• Starts from the assumption the environment is uncertain and changing
• Maps out a continuation of the present with incremental adjustments	• Relies heavily on technique of environmental scanning
• Uses technique of *backward mapping*—a desired future is envisioned, then the sequence of actions and decisions to reach that point are identified	• Builds in contingencies • Covers a period of 3 to 5 years
• Covers a period of 10 to 20 years	

Exhibit 5.2   Comparison of the Features of Long-Range and Strategic Planning

Strategic planning is especially important for nonprofit organizations with complex programs. Organizations with multiple areas of activity have specific goals and objectives for each area. One or two of these goals may be singled out for concentrated attention over two to three years because very few organizations have unlimited resources, and priorities must be set. More of an organization's resources may be applied to those goals with a high priority for a specified period of time. For example, a library wants to increase its collection, attract more users, and become a leader in information technology in the community. A major constraint to achieving any of these long-range goals is the library's overcrowded, outdated, and unsafe facility. A strategic plan to address this problem area outlines how the organization will focus its energies and resources over the next few years to resolve the issue of an inadequate facility. The library's other goals are not addressed in the strategic plan because successfully achieving them is contingent upon first resolving the facility issue.

A Board's Role in Planning

One of a nonprofit board's core responsibilities is to oversee the organization's planning. A board produces the nonprofit's long-range and strategic plans. The staff is responsible for operational plans, the working documents of an organization's various departments (e.g. marketing, community relations, fund-raising). While operational plans do not require board approval, board members should make themselves familiar with them. Small nonprofits with limited staff have little need for multiple plans. However, their long-range plans may be more detailed, include strategic issues, identify annual goals, and include operational activities associated with key objectives.

Some board members may be reluctant to participate in planning for their organization, as planning is often perceived as a tedious, time-consuming task. Planning does take time, but it is not difficult and does not have to be tedious. The process can be made much easier if each board member brings the following to the table:

- familiarity with business planning processes
- resolution to formulate a practical plan that can be implemented
- realistic expectations regarding implementation
- knowledge of where to start and when to stop
- knowledge of what questions to ask and what information is needed

- awareness that it is the big picture, not details such as the document's final form, that is important

- ability to separate the elements of a strategic or long-range plan from operational concerns.

A planning consultant can provide direction to a board that is uncertain of where or how to begin, and can help members to formulate appropriate questions about the organization's future.

All plans should include a segment on implementation. It is a board's responsibility to make sure that implementation occurs, by requesting that the executive provide periodic progress reports. Boards must accept the fact that their carefully drawn plans are not written in stone; they will need to be modified as the organization and its operating environment change. By setting aside time each year to discuss progress toward the organization's goals as described in its plan, and making any necessary adjustments, a board further ensures implementation consistent with the objectives of the plan.

Regardless of the format a board chooses for planning (e.g., standing committee, ad hoc committee, whole board), it is important that the organization's key leadership be involved. The planning process is most effective when the board and top management staff work together, as this produces dual ownership in the plan. Better results are also obtained when both the board and staff are skilled in group process techniques or are knowledgeable about the strategies for planning discussed in the following section.

Strategies for Planning

Scanning the External Environment. To effectively respond to changes, nonprofits must continually assess and interpret their environments, both internal and external. This process is called *environmental scanning*. Strategic planning emphasizes environmental scanning and captures a critical concern of today's nonprofit leadership—positioning their agencies to meet an uncertain future.

Knowledge of major social, economic, political, and technological trends enables an organization's decisionmakers to anticipate change and adjust direction accordingly. It is important to know, for example, if the community served by the organization is projecting population and economic growth or decline. The fact that U.S. society is aging (baby boomers are now in their fifties) affects organizations' service and donor targets. The advent of the Internet and other technological advances has significantly affected the way all organizations do business. Nonprofits must be prepared for all types of changes. More nonprofits might follow the aggressive marketing lead of PAWS, an animal shelter in Lynnwood, Washington, which has created a "virtual shelter" via a home page on the Internet. People can list adoptable animals, shop for a pet, search for a lost pet, learn how to care for their pet, determine which apartments for rent are pet friendly, and more by logging on to PAWS' Internet address.

External environmental scanning requires the evaluation of large amounts of data. Fortunately, this information is readily accessible through a variety of agencies (e.g., school districts, state planning agencies, public and university libraries, professional associations, banks, chambers of commerce).

A first step for an organization in scanning its external environment is to determine what type of information is needed. But the more critical step is to make sense of the data. What might it mean to an organization that school enrollments have declined, the local economy is flat, or elected officials are challenging tax laws that govern exempt property? Those trends likely to have the greatest impact on the organization may direct the planning group to set new goals. The "9-Box Tool" (see Appendix E) is a popular technique groups have used to access their members' perceptions about trends. It is important that the benefits from assessing the external environment be shared with the planning group, so that the persons involved in data collection and analysis can see the value of their contribution. External environmental scanning produces information critical to an organization's growth or survival, and enables the alert organization to act on perceived threats in a timely manner. Other benefits include:

- The opportunity for an organization's planning group to view the organization in relationship to its environment and acquire the skills to interact with that environment.
- The reduction of uncertainty and increased preparedness for change.
- The ability to better satisfy key (external) stakeholders through increased understanding of their concerns.
- Reversal of an organization's natural tendency to look inward.[6]

The Shriners organization provides an example of the value of assessing the external environment. The group's governing body recognized the need to reexamine the organization's role in society when faced with recent declines in membership. The Shriners Imperial Council hired the national research and polling firm of Louis Harris and Associates in to conduct a national survey to determine the values and attitudes of American men between the ages of thirty-five and fifty-five regarding their use of leisure time, and specifically about belonging to a fraternal organization. Some of the research findings were supportive of the Shriners' existing policies, and some were not. For example, whereas 76 percent of the respondents were involved in volunteer or community activities, 47 percent reported having difficulty finding enough leisure time for themselves or to spend with their families. It also was determined that men in this demographic group were not interested in belonging to organizations that accepted only male members and wanted an organization's dress code "left unspecified." [7] It was concluded that many features of the Shriners' fraternal organization, such as male-only membership and distinctive dress, were unappealing to today's men.

The findings suggest that if the Shriners are to continue to attract new members, they will have to market membership differently, find new membership targets, adjust their membership policies, and possibly realign the way Shriners Temples conduct their affairs. Some Shriners' traditions have already been adjusted in response to members' changing values. With the exception of the swearing-in ceremony, ceremonials previously reserved for the membership only are now open to families.

In response to this feedback, the Shriners have asked themselves some hard questions about their heritage and mission. As the Imperial Council stated, "We must face the answers unflinchingly, and take appropriate steps to restore the prestige which the Shrine has enjoyed over the years. . . . It will not be easy, however, and will need the concentrated efforts of all of us to get it done." [8]

Scanning the Internal Environment.   An assessment inside an organization involves identifying factors that either facilitate or hinder fulfillment of its mission. According to systems theory, an organization operating as an open system depends on its external environment for both the acquisition of resources and acceptance of its output (product or service). Assuming a nonprofit operates as an open system, it needs to examine three elements: the organization's resources (input), its current strategies and processes, and its performance (output).

The board of directors is presumably made up of individuals representing different constituencies in the community, and therefore should be better suited to assess the external environment. However, a board is part time, and this condition constrains its ability to conduct a thorough scanning and analysis. Conversely, the staff is most knowledgeable about an organization's operations and programs, and therefore should be better suited to assess the internal environment. However, staff may be too close to the organization to conduct an objective scanning and analysis. For example, they may be so accustomed to working around obstacles and making do with inadequate resources that they ignore what an outsider would identify as a weakness in the organization's operations. Because a board can learn from (temporarily) stepping inside the organization for a closer look, and staff can learn from looking outside the organization, boards and staff should work together on environmental scanning activities. In most cases a board of directors would be responsible for ensuring that environmental scanning is part of its strategic planning process. Two types of environmental scanning are SWOT analysis and on-site analysis.

SWOT analysis. A strengths, weaknesses, opportunities, and threats (SWOT) analysis is one method for assessing an organization's environment and is an important phase of a strategic planning process that can reveal strategic issues, or issues that connect the internal functions of an organization to the larger external context in which it operates. The primary purposes of a SWOT analysis are (1) to alert an organization's members to potential opportunities or threats from the environment, and (2) to enable the organization to respond effectively by drawing upon identified strengths. An organization that acknowledges its weaknesses and works to correct them will be in a better position to minimize the impact of external threats and ward off potential crises.

A focus group made up of the organization's primary stakeholders can be used to develop a SWOT list. The planning group should analyze the SWOT findings and use this information as one basis for setting or prioritizing goals and planning a course of action.

On-site analysis. When groups learn how to approach decision-making and problem-solving situations effectively, they are better equipped to deal with strategic planning. The United Way of the Lower Mainland (Vancouver) in British Columbia uses a process called "on-site analysis" to assist agencies in group problem solving and decision making. On-site analysis training, which refers to analyzing operations at the workplace, has been implemented successfully in more than two thousand agencies in Canada, the United States, and Australia. According to the Executive Director of the United Way of the Lower Mainland, a key component of on-site analysis is its focus on factual decision making. "Groups need to step back from their *perceptions* about what is happening [in an organization] and what needs to happen. They need *factual reality*."

> The primary goal of on-site analysis is to bring about an environment in which change to improve organizational performance and effectiveness can occur. This includes an analysis of strengths and problems, and steps to enhance the strengths and solve the problems. It results in a staff team who clearly understand the current situation and are committed to do something to improve it. . . . These primary goals are achieved through a group problem-solving process which includes a rigorous, fact-based assessment of exactly what the organization is doing at the time of the analysis and what it has been doing over the previous three-to-five years. Areas of greatest potential for improvement are identified by the group, and those agreed to be most important become the focus for the remaining steps of the process.[9]

The type of factual review provided by on-site analysis changes the level of debate, equalizes knowledge, enables priorities to be grounded in reality, and empowers the board to deal effectively with functional issues. Knowing the facts also reduces the potential for conflict that can emerge when members have different perceptions and expectations of their organization.[10]

FISCAL MATTERS AND FUND-RAISING

A nonprofit board of directors has several related responsibilities in the area of finances. These include:

- Establishment of fiscal policies to direct the way the organization acquires and uses financial resources; policies that deal with limitations on expenditures and/or indebtedness; investment priorities; ethical fund-raising practices; and standards of accounting.
- Approval of the organization's budget.
- Establishment of a process for monitoring the fiscal affairs of the organization.
- Assistance in raising funds for the organization.
- Making contributions.

Boards differ in their degree of involvement in these various functions; the key variable is staff expertise. As with other matters pertaining to nonprofit operations, the fewer the number of staff, the greater the likelihood that board members will assume a hands-on approach to managing the organization's financial affairs.

Budgeting and the Board

An organization's budget states in numbers what an organization's plans say in words. The budget is the means for meeting an organization's goals, and it is the fundamental tool for controlling an organization's fiscal activities and allocating its resources. For these reasons, the budgeting process must be based on a full understanding of the details of the programs it supports. Consequently, budget preparation should be an administrative staff responsibility.

Many nonprofit organizations use a board finance or budget committee to plan the organization's budget line by line. Because board members usually do not have full knowledge of the organization's day-to-day operations, they cannot know how much it costs to run a program without staff input. A committee-driven budgeting process creates more work for an executive, and produces a budget by a group of individuals who do not have to operate within it. There are several benefits to involving staff in creating the organization's budget:

- They can see how their respective areas of responsibility fit into the whole.
- They are more apt to consider the budget when making spending decisions.
- Their accountability is increased.

However, a board should not simply rubber-stamp a budget presented to them by the executive. The board's role is to ask questions to ensure that the budget is realistic and reflects the organization's mission and plans. Many board members are not familiar with the fund accounting standards used by nonprofit organizations. Before a board is asked to review and approve a budget, the executive and board chairperson should discuss ways to educate new members on how to interpret nonprofit budgets and financial statements.

Fiscal Oversight Responsibilities of a Board

A nonprofit board is responsible for monitoring the fiscal health of its organization. To do this systematically, a set of key indicators of fiscal health should be established. A board should know the answers to the following general questions:

1. Is the organization in financial equilibrium? Do financial reports show a balance between income and expenditures?

2. If the organization has a capital funds account, is it growing at a sufficient rate to meet future needs? Are withdrawals being made from this account to pay noncapital expenditures (e.g., operating costs, deferred maintenance)?

3. Is the organization's fund-raising success (or lack of success) comparable to that of similar organizations? What is the organization's record of fund-raising in the areas of operating and capital funds?

4. Is the organization financially vulnerable to changes in the external resource environment (e.g., shifts in donors' priorities, reduction in government spending, increased competition)? To what extent are the sources of funds diversified?

5. If the organization has an endowment, are the invested funds performing according to expectations?

6. Are the organization's assets accessible in the event of some financial crisis?

7. Does the organization have a deficit? Are there explicit plans for servicing or retiring the debt?[11]

A Board's Fund-Raising Role

There seem to be many misconceptions about what fund-raising is, how it is done, and who is responsible for it. Misconceptions aside, nonprofit boards are ultimately responsible for their organizations' financial resources and this is a matter of great concern for many nonprofit boards.

The 1994 survey of the National Center for Nonprofit Boards (NCNB) reported that executives most often cited their boards' "lack of fund-raising capability and lack of commitment and involvement" as a major weakness; less than 5 percent of the respondents cited fund-raising as a board strength.[12] It also was found that 71 percent of the responding organizations did not have policies that addressed board members' personal contributions; 59 percent of those who did were organizations in the field of arts and culture, compared to 32 percent in the field of human services, 27 percent in education, and 23 percent in the field of health. Eighty percent of the board members of arts and cultural organizations surveyed made contributions to their organizations, which correlates with the fact that these organizations also were more likely to have policies on board contributions.

The reason so many nonprofit organizations' boards may not be involved in fund-raising or in making personal contributions is that they are not asked. Requesting assistance is obviously a first step, but because many nonprofit board members may not have had prior fund-raising experience, the chief executive or development director should help to educate the board in fund-raising strategies. A colleague and fund-raising consultant tells boards, "Fund-raising is not rocket science; you need someone to lead the charge, you need the executive to be involved, and you need to give it time." [13] Successful fund-raising requires patience, persistence, the ability to target appropriate donors, and a worthwhile cause. This latter point is very important. Fund-raisers must be fully committed to their organizations' missions; if they are not, their hesitancy will probably be apparent. An enthusiastic attitude produces a far greater response from prospective donors than an apologetic or half-hearted one.

Attitudes and perceptions can affect the choice of strategies for pursuing financial support. During new board member orientation some time should be set aside to discuss members' feelings about money, fund-raising, personal solicitations, and their experiences in raising funds. Once board members' attitudes on fund-raising are revealed and discussed, the board should establish a philosophy of fund development as a basis for setting appropriate policies to guide fund-raising activities.

Answering the following questions can assist a board in developing fund-raising policies:

- What is the board willing to do to help the organization raise money?
- Do board members feel that the ends justify the means in the pursuit of funds for a worthy cause?
- Is there a bias toward or against seeking government grants or contracts or funds from a specific source?
- Are there objections to earning funds through an entrepreneurial endeavor?
- Are there objections to charging fees for services?

- Would the board be willing to collaborate with other organizations in fund-raising?

Some very good board members may never be effective solicitors. Others may feel more comfortable soliciting in-kind goods and services than making direct appeals for money. Board members can contribute to their organization's overall fund development efforts in many ways, such as:

- supply lists of prospects
- arrange appointments with prospects
- use their influence to help open doors for development staff
- make follow-up phone calls
- host social gatherings for donors or prospects
- add personal notes to letters of appeal
- present awards to donors
- make presentations to prospects.

Some nonprofits have clout or an easily identifiable donor constituency but many do not. It is important to set realistic fund-raising goals based on an organization's capacity to raise funds. Nonprofits with limited fund-raising capacity must evaluate their options, including the following:

1. Trim operations so expenses are aligned with potential income.
2. Increase fund-raising capacity by, for example, adding a new mix of people to the board or staff, focusing on increased visibility and public image, and strategically addressing whatever constrains the ability to raise funds.
3. Explore income-generating programs, service fees, or unrelated business income.
4. Consider either collaborative fund-raising or a merger. (Chapter 9 discusses collaboration and mergers.)

The Impact of Changes in the Resource Environment

Changes in the social and economic environment impact nonprofit organizations' ability to raise funds. According to a former foundation official and board member of Independent Sector, three trends have converged to create a new climate in the resource environment for nonprofits:

1. There has been phenomenal growth in the number of nonprofit organizations. In 1940, the IRS estimated that there were 12,000 charitable tax-exempt organizations nationwide; in 1992, that number exceeded 1.2 million.[14] In the tricounty area of Detroit, Michigan, the total number of nonprofits with at least one employee, in the fields of education, social services, health, recreation, and arts (excluding colleges and universities and hospitals) more than doubled from 1982 to 1992.[15] From 1988 to 1994, the number of federally tax-exempt organizations in Washington State increased by almost 300 percent.[16] A greater number of nonprofit organizations means more competition for funding, public attention, volunteers, and experienced nonprofit board members.

2. There is a growing perception that further cuts in government social welfare spending will result in increased help from private citizens.[17] Those who profess this viewpoint are unaware of the fact that American charity is no longer based upon neighbor helping neighbor. Instead, it is an array of organizations largely run by professionals, many of which are highly dependent on government grants and contracts. It is so far unclear whether tougher rules for welfare and other social services will reduce or expand the need for such services.

3. Private-sector giving has flattened out. Foundation grants increased by 6.56 percent from 1992 to 1993, a 2.57 percent increase when adjusted for inflation. Corporate giving in both 1992 and 1993 was $5.92 billion; after adjustment for inflation, this represents a decrease of 3.75 percent. Individual philanthropy was $99.18 billion in 1992 and $102.55 billion in 1993, a decrease of 0.47 percent after inflation.[18] Traditional sources of private-sector funding have not kept pace with demand and represent only a fraction of the government's capacity to provide financial support to nonprofit organizations.

In light of these trends, nonprofits must change their fund-raising strategies and targets. Depending on traditional foundation and corporate resources is not likely to pay handsome dividends. Nonprofits need to be more cooperative, creative, entrepreneurial, and strategically oriented to survive in the new fund-raising environment. They need to collaborate rather than become more competitive in order to generate new sources of revenue. Nonprofits should consider how they can align themselves with others in the same field, using their cooperation as leverage for attracting new sources to support their mutual service areas. The result can be a broadened funding base for the organizations involved.

New fund-raising targets include small and medium-sized businesses, newly emerging family foundations, and new pooled funds from donors of moderate means. For example, the Fidelity Investment Company of Boston created a nonprofit Charitable Gifts Fund in 1992, which allows donors to pool their investments and designate a portion of the Fund's earning to charitable organizations. The parent company provides management and investment services, but the donors decide which nonprofits receive contributions. In only three years, the Charitable Fund has disbursed approximately $125 million to over ten thousand nonprofit organizations.[19]

Even more recent fund-raising strategies include: solicitation of matching funds from new sources, efforts to turn impulse giving from direct mail appeals into on-going gifts through direct debit transactions, marketing through the Internet, and cause-related marketing. In cause-related marketing a company donates a percentage of the price of some product to charity. For example, 1 percent of the sales of Ben & Jerry's™ ice cream goes to peace projects. Since 1982, Newman's Own™ foods has donated all profits to charity. Coupon programs also are a common cause-marketing program, under which a company gives ten to fifteen cents to some specific charity per coupon redeemed. Critics say companies substitute cause-marketing for corporate philanthropy, and that they are more interested in using a charitable cause for their own good public image than they are in helping the charity.[20]

The composition of nonprofit boards of directors and the degree to which board members are connected in their communities will make a difference in the new fund-raising environment. Over the last two decades, many nonprofits relied more on professional fund-raising staff than on their boards to raise funds. This makes sense when government, foundation, and corporate grants are primary sources of funds. However, if nonprofits are to successfully target new sources, the activity of cultivating prospects once again becomes critical. The relationships and ties a board has within the community will become increasingly important. Board members will be expected to cultivate owners of small (50 or fewer employees) and medium-sized (50 to 250 employees) businesses rather than the CEOs of big corporations and major foundations. Since the cultivation of prospects is proven to be more effective on a peer level, this function is more appropriate to a board than to fund-raising staff.

Yet another change of concern to nonprofit organizations is the evolving demographics of U.S. society. Just as the twenty-first century will increasingly reflect the traditions and values of groups such as Asian Americans, African Americans, Hispanic Americans, and Native Americans, a larger percentage of charitable donors will be from these groups. If a nonprofit organization expects to receive support from such donor groups, a diversified staff and board of directors is mandatory. James Joseph, President and CEO of the Council on Foundations, suggests that the newly emerging majority is likely to redefine America's civic culture. Nonprofit boards will need to "understand the many ways in which the boundaries of community are changing," including changing traditions of private benevolence.[21]

SUGGESTIONS FOR FURTHER READING

Herman, Robert D., and J. Van Til, eds. *Nonprofit Boards of Directors: Analyses and Applications.* New Brunswick: Transaction Books, 1989.

Jacob, M.E.L. *Strategic Planning: A How-To-Do-It Manual for Librarians.* New York: Neal-Schuman Publishers, 1990. (Note: Although written for a library audience, this manual is applicable to a much broader audience.)

Pfeiffer, J.W., L.D. Goodstein, and T.M. Nolan. *Applied Strategic Planning: A How To Do It Guide.* San Diego: University Associates, 1986.

Witkin, Belle Ruth, and James W. Altschuld. *Planning and Conducting Needs Assessments: A Practical Guide.* Thousand Oaks: Sage Publications, 1995.

CHAPTER SIX

Building a Cooperative Spirit

mpowerment has become a buzzword of the 1990s. To empower means to give power or authority to someone, to enable or permit. Individuals and groups are empowered when they are provided with different options for establishing self-control or control of some situation, and the means for implementing their options.

Nonprofit boards of directors are empowered when they are provided the means for governing effectively. Nonprofit executives are empowered when they are given the authority to manage effectively. In an ideal situation both the board and the executive are empowered to perform their respective functions, and the use of options to achieve mutual goals is the norm. This chapter examines the board-executive relationship, communication between nonprofit boards and executives as a source of empowerment, and different means for fulfilling their respective leadership roles. Human resource management in the boardroom also is explored, including the pivotal role of the board chairperson in facilitating a climate of cooperation among board members. The chapter concludes with a case study illustrating effective relationships among the executive, board, and staff of a California service organization.

PERSPECTIVES ON BOARD-EXECUTIVE RELATIONSHIPS

Over the past twenty to thirty years, different schools of thought regarding the nonprofit board-executive relationship have prevailed. Some professed that the executive should be in control of the board, while others said the board should be dominant and the proper role of the executive should be to manage the organization according to board directives. Neither of these dichotomous approaches has proven to be effective over time. One alternative is that a board and an executive can share the responsibilities of governance, but this approach can lead to confusion, as lines of authority become blurred. The following examples demonstrate that nonprofits continue to struggle to find a comfortable and effective board-executive relationship.

- The chief executive of a Canadian United Way states that there are too many nonprofit executives who do not accord their boards of directors the kind of importance they deserve: "These executives see their board as something they simply have to put up with. They feel their real job is providing services, not managing a board. It is these same executives who also tend to complain about how bad their board is. Nonprofit executives need to recognize that the board is also one of their responsibilities." [1]

- The chairperson of the board of directors of an animal shelter has literally ruled the organization for more than fourteen years. The chair's dominant and abrasive personality has caused excessive turnover among board members and staff, and the organization has difficulty attracting quality staff and volunteers. Most board members recognize that the board needs positive leadership, but no one is willing to assume the responsibility. The chief executive's attempts to educate board members regarding their roles and options have been blocked by the board chair.

- The chief executive of a women's shelter attempted to dominate the board by refusing to be a team player; she failed to recognize her accountability to the board. To protect her ownership of the organization, she engaged in behaviors such as withholding critical information from the board of directors, misrepresenting the nature and extent of the organization's programs, and presenting inaccurate audit reports to the board for approval. After several unsuccessful attempts at finding a *zone of accommodation* (area of compromise) with the executive, the board fired her.

Whenever a board of directors has reason to suspect that its organization is not operating according to its plans, or is deviating from its mission and goals in some way, it should not hesitate to step into a more administrative role, at least temporarily, until corrections are made. By the same token, the chief executive should not hesitate to speak up if the board is overstepping its bounds without apparent cause. The board-executive relationship should be a dynamic one, in which roles are adapted to the changing needs of the organization. The primary concern should be the effective functioning of the organization rather than who is in control.

Organizations and their primary players change over time, resulting in shifts in power and control. There may be times when there is a balanced relationship between the executive and the board, and times when one or the other dominates. The following sections outline three different ways to approach the board-executive relationship that are appropriate for today's complex nonprofit organizations: executive focus, balanced partnership, and strong board/strong executive. While these different approaches describe existing board-executive relationships, they also may serve as models for change.

Executive Focus on Board Behaviors

In a study of fifty nonprofit executives with reputations for being highly effective, Robert Herman and Richard Heimovics found that the basis for effectiveness was leadership behavior in relationship to their boards of directors.[2] They called this trait *board-regarding behaviors*. These effective nonprofit executives focused their leadership actions more toward the board than the staff and tended to practice the following principles:

1. Create an environment conducive to quality board interaction. An effective executive does not stand aside and just let the board operate on its own. The executive is actively involved in seeing that board members are satisfied and productive as individuals and as a group.

2. View the board-executive relationship as an exchange. An effective executive takes the time to meet with board members one-on-one to learn the skills they bring to the organization, their interests, their motivations for serving on the board, and so forth. The executive makes a concerted effort to show respect toward each member of the board.

3. Work with the board in an entrepreneurial manner. An executive has the capacity to envision change and innovation and inspire the board to the same type of vision.

4. Keep the board of directors informed with timely information and materials relevant to its decision making.

5. Work closely with the board chairperson and committee chairs to promote board productivity.[3]

The premise of the study was the idea that the effectiveness of a nonprofit organization depends on its ability to manage the changing demands and constraints of its resource environment, a concept called *resource dependency*. A board of directors plays a significant role in mediating the nonprofit's dependency on its resource environment in the sense that members may be recruited based on their ability to give money and attract resources, or assist in developing new sources of funds. Effective nonprofit executives work: "with and through their boards to position their organizations in a changing resource environment in order to stabilize operations and/or facilitate growth and development."[4] Therefore, from a resource dependency perspective, a board is responsible for strategic mediation of the organization's external environment, and the executive facilitates this role. In order to accomplish this, an executive: (1) keeps board members well informed of shifts in the environment and trends that could impact the organization (e.g., funding cutbacks); (2) is alert to changing circumstances that offer potential for innovation (e.g., mergers and collaboration); and (3) encourages the board to consider new and better ways for carrying out its fiduciary responsibilities.

A Balanced Partnership

Whereas the executive-focus model perceives the board-executive relationship as an exchange, the concept of a partnership implies interdependence and equally shared responsibilities. Applied to a nonprofit board of directors, a partnership-type relationship with the executive emphasizes explicitly assigned roles for each partner, mutual trust, and understanding. The distinctions between the functions of a board and those of an executive will not always be clear, producing a constant state of tension. In a healthy organization, this tension is dynamic; it prompts continual dialogue about the way the organization conducts (or could conduct) its business.

Along with trust comes the freedom to disagree. Both the board and the executive need to recognize issues on which they disagree and respect the other's opinion, while at the same time working toward a zone of accommodation. Board-executive relationships evolve; it takes time to learn one another's strengths and weaknesses, values, and points of contention. Trust and respect are cornerstones of a good working partnership, but the ability to compromise also is important.

Boards of directors and executives have opposing influences on organizations because they work from different frames of reference; these differences also can serve to balance out their relationships. Exhibit 6.1 illustrates

• Executives are paid	• Boards are volunteers
• Executives are full time	• Boards are part time
• Executives are singularly committed to their organization; it's their job and/or career	• Board members have to choose between commitments; members typically serve on more than one board
• Executives are individuals	• Boards are corporate
• Executives can make decisions alone	• Boards make only group decisions
• Executives have a staff	• Boards do not have staff
• Executives are temporary	• Boards (as an entity) are permanent
• Executives are professionals in the organization's area of service	• Boards are typically non experts
• Executives' responsibilities are limited and immediate	• Boards have the ultimate responsibility for an organization

Exhibit 6.1   Frames of Reference of Executives and Boards of Directors

the contrasting frames of reference of executives and boards of directors. Acknowledging and respecting these differences helps to keep the board-executive relationship in perspective.

Strong Boards and Strong Executives

Some studies of nonprofit organizations show that more effective organizations have a strong board *and* a strong executive. As one United Way executive put it, "A strong board wouldn't tolerate a weak executive; and if you have a strong executive you will probably also have a strong board." [5] This model differs from the concept of a balanced partnership, which emphasizes a lack of dominance by either the board or the executive. Perhaps this is a subtle distinction, but it is an important one. For example, a weak (unempowered) board and a weak executive could be a balanced board-executive relationship because neither would be dominant.

Effecting a strong board/strong executive relationship begins with a clear definition of the job functions of the board and the executive. The use of the term *job function* (rather than responsibility) is significant, as it emphasizes a broader viewpoint. Some nonprofits consider activities when outlining the respective responsibilities of their boards and staffs (e.g., staff members write proposals, board members sell benefit tickets). This approach, sometimes perceived as sharing or balancing board-staff responsibilities, calls undue attention to details. The following quote from Carver expresses a more appropriate way to think about delineating board-executive functions that can lead to a strong board/strong executive relationship.

> The effective board relationship with an executive is one that recognizes that job products of board and executive are truly separate. Effectiveness calls for two strong, totally different responsibilities. Either party trying to do the other's job is interfering with effective operation. It is not the board's task to save the chief executive from the responsibilities of that job nor is it the chief executive's task to save the board from the responsibilities of governing. Further, who works for whom must always remain clear. The board can respect, even revere, the chief executive's skills, commitment, and leadership, yet never slip subtly into acting as if the board works for him or her.[6]

According to Carver's governance model (discussed in Chapter 1 and Chapter 5), once a board has established *end* policies and *executive limitation* policies, it has empowered the executive by providing the means for implementing realistic options and should not interfere in operational matters. This does not mean that a board should never have contact with any of the organization's staff, or never share ideas about the program; such rigidity is obviously too limiting. For example, termination of a staff member other than the executive, or the choice of a location for the annual fundraising dinner are lower-level staff decisions out of a board's purview.

The following example illustrates an appropriate board response to an operations problem. An arts organization hired a new receptionist who was curt on the phone and frequently failed to pass board members' messages to the executive. The board was tempted to terminate her employment but knew this was an inappropriate board action. Instead, the board chairperson spoke to the executive on behalf of the board and shared their feelings about the receptionist. Within a few weeks, the receptionist was replaced.

Another example demonstrates the type of problem executives can experience if they are not fully empowered by their boards to carry out the mandates of their positions. The executive of a large community action agency manages approximately twenty-six different government contracts that support the agency's programs. One of the agency's largest, most complex and costly programs is its countywide transportation program for the elderly and disabled. The board hired the executive to administer this multimillion dollar nonprofit but had not empowered her with sufficient authority. For example, the agency received a request for proposal (RFP) from a regional transportation district. The RFP had a three week deadline. At the time, agency policy required board approval of all contract bids. However, the deadline did not allow time for the executive to both write up the bid and adequately prepare the board for this critical decision. Consequently, the agency lost the opportunity to compete for this contract. As a result of this incident, the executive asked the board to (1) set parameters regarding contract bids, (2) specify the types of contracts the staff could solicit, and (3) outline the conditions under which the staff could go forward without board approval. The executive now has the capacity to optimize her leadership, and the board-executive relationship has been strengthened by this clarification of roles.

Effective Communication

A key factor in establishing effective communication between a board and an executive is mutual awareness of one another's roles. The expectations associated with each role need to be explicit. The way those roles are defined will influence styles of communication (formal versus informal), communication processes (one-on-one or group, written or oral), and content. Board-executive communications are more complicated than executive-staff or internal board communications because an executive is communicating from one perspective, whereas a board of directors represents many perspectives but communicates as if it were of one voice. It is important that a board be consistent in its communications with the executive, who may otherwise become frustrated by mixed messages.

If a board and executive are to develop effective communication, it is important for them not only to clarify their respective roles and expectations, but also to discover the reasons behind their positions. For example, uncovering the basis for an individual's position on an issue may lead the board or executive to supply additional information, correct misperceptions, or present information in a different way in order to resolve differences.

HUMAN RESOURCE MANAGEMENT IN THE BOARDROOM

Most boards are more concerned with issues and content than processes of communication and interpersonal relationships. The better developed the relationships among board members, the greater the cooperation and work toward common goals. The basis of effective interpersonal relationships is clearly communicated expectations. When someone's behavior does not match up to the expectations of the executive, board chair, or majority of other members, board interpersonal relationships are weakened.

Relationships evolve over time based on *norms of reciprocity.* Reciprocity is essential to positive relationships among board members. If it is lacking, the effectiveness of the board and the organization is jeopardized. For example, in one nonprofit there was virtually no sense of reciprocity; board members lacked respect for one another and for the staff. The board did little to guide the organization or monitor its activities, and the executive did nothing to help the board fulfill its governance responsibilities. Over time, the staff developed the perception that the board was incompetent, not trustworthy, and lacked a genuine concern about the fate of the organization. The board responded in kind and behaved as the staff expected, a self-fulfilling prophecy. In this case, a lack of reciprocity among board members and in the board-staff relationship led to a dysfunctional board and organization.

All groups must address issues such as morale, participation, the existence of conflict or competition between group members, and the level and consistency of cooperation. Effective interpersonal relationships can usually be found within groups whose members interact freely, are interdependent, and have respect for one another. The chairperson plays a key role in strengthening the interpersonal relationships of the board.

The Role of the Chairperson

An effective chairperson has the ability to create a unified and cohesive board from a group of individuals with different needs, expectations, and personalities. He or she takes the initiative in helping the board fulfill its obligations and fosters loyalty to the organization's mission. Management of diversity also is important to:

> Create and maintain a spirit of unity among the diverse people on the board and to ensure that it works appropriately with the executive and staff in exercising power effectively and ethically. . . . It is the chairman's task to lead and to motivate, to blend in proper proportion the more capable and vocal members with the less experienced and silent ones.[7]

The chairperson should focus on the effective operation of the board—its structure, work habits, decision making, and interpersonal relationships. The strength of a chairperson is reflected in the effectiveness of the board; the best leaders are able to recognize and develop leadership potential from their groups. Ironically, for those better boards that take great care in choosing a chairperson with appropriate and requisite skills, strong leadership emanating from the chair is less important (at least in the short term).[8]

The chairperson of the board is expected, among other things, to do the following:

- work closely with the executive
- set meeting agendas, call meetings, and preside over them
- resolve disputes and manage conflict among board members
- assign members to committees or specific tasks
- act as principal spokesperson for the board
- keep the board fully informed about board business
- orchestrate goal setting for the board
- clarify members' roles and responsibilities
- ensure a process for board members' orientation, training, development, and evaluation
- motivate members
- plan for evaluation of the executive.

This is an enormous undertaking requiring a great deal of commitment. How an individual actually handles the many responsibilities that go with being chairperson depends on the board's norms (how it has conducted its business in the past), any organizational circumstances that may make special demands on the board (e.g., whether it is stable or unstable, expanding or contracting), and the chair's personal style of leadership.

Management of Conflict

The nature of nonprofit organizations and the diverse people they bring together makes some conflict inevitable. All groups at some time are forced to deal with the problem of dissent. Diversity and dissent can be productive in a board setting, because they stimulate discussion and problem solving. One nonprofit executive worries more about a board that is continually congenial and agreeable on every issue than one that expresses conflicting opinions: "I want to be sure that the board is weighing different views, the pros and cons of an issue, and expressing what they strongly believe." [9]

A board member who expresses a different viewpoint can force others to clarify their positions, which, in turn, can lead to a broader understanding of the issue at hand. Someone whose persistence may cause him to be seen as a nitpicker, for example, may simply be trying to make a point for change. A devil's advocate can keep a board from becoming complacent by forcing other members to reexamine their thinking.

Unfortunately, if differences of opinion are taken personally, disagreements can deteriorate into conflict among individual board members or between the board and the executive. It is important to try to determine the reasons for discord. A board's leadership plays a major role in helping to keep conflict impersonal and disagreements healthy. A board chairperson might consider the following options to diffuse conflict:

- Ask for different opinions on an issue even when there appears to be complete agreement. This gives permission to the individual who may be suppressing disagreement to bring concerns out in the open.

- Disassociate an idea from the individual who offers it. Ask, "What do you think of the suggestion to. . . ." rather than, "What is your reaction to Sue's idea?" This avoids disagreements on a personal level.

- Redirect the discussion back to the issues at hand when personal attacks are made during a meeting.

- Adhere to the rules of effective meetings (see Chapter 7).

Ideally, group leaders manage conflict in a way that facilitates the group process and does not interfere with the business of the group. However, this is not an easy task. If a group refuses to respond to efforts at conciliation, use of an outside mediator may be necessary. The board of one youth-services organization found that using an outside mediator when it had reached an impasse on an issue helped it to move forward. During the course of this organization's annual planning efforts, conflict emerged over certain goals and directions; the board planning committee was unable to move past these differences. A volunteer mediator from another nonprofit agency helped the committee to find a way around its trouble spot, resulting in a long-range plan acceptable to all parties.

RECIPROCITY IN PRACTICE: A CASE STUDY

Girls Incorporated of Greater Santa Barbara has been in operation for approximately thirty-five years. In 1990, it changed its name from the Girls Club of Santa Barbara to Girls Incorporated in order to retain its emphasis on programming for girls at the time when Boys and Girls Clubs nationwide were merging. The organization presently employs approximately fifty full- and part-time staff, with up to sixty staff members during the summer months; its budget is $1.2 million.

The chief executive of Girls Incorporated of Greater Santa Barbara has been with the agency for five years, and previously served as the executive for another Girls Club organization for nearly fifteen years; she is an astute individual when it comes to managing a volunteer board of directors. She is soft-spoken but persuasive, sensitive, responsive, and a dynamic leader. It is evident that she also thoroughly enjoys working with people.

She describes the relationship with her current board of directors as positive and unique because the board takes the time to show appreciation for the staff and herself. (This has not been her experience with all boards.) She describes the board as "an intelligent group; they pay attention, they read the materials I send out in advance and come to meetings prepared." This executive works hard to create a positive board-executive relationship. She acknowledges the work of the board and of individual members, sends them personal thank-you notes, recognizes members in front of their peers, and includes a personalized update on her activities with the monthly board mailings.

To facilitate good relations between the board and the rest of her staff, at every other board meeting she showcases one of the organization's programs; the basic objectives of a program and what it is designed to achieve are revisited, and board members are given a hands-on experience. For example, they may participate in an activity similar to what the girls are doing or watch a video of a program in action. This approach has enhanced board-staff relationships because it has helped board members to better understand all Girls Incorporated program areas and the role of staff in implementing the organization's mission. Good board-staff relationships are reciprocal. The staff helps to educate the board of directors to enable them to make better decisions about policies and financial matters.

Another important factor in the executive's relationship with the board is that she focuses on the presentation of facts:

> I don't try to influence their decisions. If they ask for my opinion I give it, but I don't try to make my opinion more important than theirs. I see myself as a facilitator in the board's decision-making process. My experience has shown that if I accurately define a problem and accurately identify available resources, there really aren't that many possible solutions. It is better for them [the board] to find a solution than for me to come with the problem, the resources, and the solution.

With more than twenty years' experience, this executive has learned to adapt to a wide range of board leadership styles. "Some board presidents have really wanted to be active in a hands-on kind of way; others just want to chair meetings or be in the forefront. Either way has worked, but I need to be ready to step aside when I have a president who wants to be more involved." When busy professional people are board chairs, their time is very limited. She has found that when everything is prepared for them in advance, they can do a good job, although it takes more time and energy on her part. The best thing about having a board of directors is access to their expertise. "I am very grateful for the free advice from a wide range of professional people. I didn't realize how important this was until I went to work in the private sector for a few years. For one thing, I realized the cost attached to acquiring expertise. In a nonprofit organization, I can access so much expertise; it's just a phone call away!" [10]

SUGGESTIONS FOR FURTHER READING

Hunt, Gary T. *Communication Skills in the Organization.* Englewood Cliffs: Prentice-Hall Publishers, 1980.

Kreps, Gary L. *Organizational Communication,* 2nd ed. New York: Longman Publishers, 1990.

CHAPTER SEVEN

Effective Board Meetings

M eetings are the primary method used by boards of directors to fulfill their governance responsibilities; they should thus be meaningful, thoughtfully planned, and well run in order for boards to be productive. In addition, members must approach meetings seriously and be prepared to devote their full attention to the agenda. A casual board meeting that approximates a social gathering and does not deal with issues in a serious way will produce inferior decisions and may leave the board vulnerable to *judicial review* (legal liability).[1]

The first part of this chapter discusses the principles of good meetings, and explores ways to construct agendas and conduct meetings in order to make the best use of the board's time. The second part is devoted to effective decision making, and presents ideas for maximizing board members' participation in meetings.

THE IMPORTANCE OF MEETINGS

A board of directors is a collection of individuals with different insights, perspectives, knowledge, and spheres of influence; these differences are valuable resources for the organization. Meetings give boards their collective identity because they offer the opportunity for members to exchange information and test, argue, and refine their ideas. Board and committee meetings are also significant as the only forum in which board members can carry out their collective responsibilities. A theater board does not direct plays any more than a day care center board takes care of children. Instead, a board's job is verbal and its tools are words.[2] A board deliberates, clarifies, analyzes, and problem solves:

> When the job is one of words, there must be discipline in the talking. That discipline involves *what* is talked about, *how* the talking occurs, and *when* it is done. It is not acceptable to talk about any issue that might come up. It is not acceptable to talk about an issue in whatever way desired. It is not acceptable to talk about an issue at an inappropriate time. . . . When boards wander aimlessly, they are as negligent as the professional shortstop who decides that right field is a nicer place to be today.[3]

This does not mean that meetings should be all work and no play—a bit of levity helps to maintain equilibrium. But board members must concentrate on matters related to their governance responsibilities in order to maintain their effectiveness as a group.

Productive board meetings also can be a source of satisfaction to board members, which is important in maintaining their motivation and commitment. Board members are rewarded by seeing how they fit into the larger organizational picture and how their contributions as members of the board help the organization achieve its goals.

PRINCIPLES OF EFFECTIVE MEETINGS

Effective meetings depend on the quality of relationships among the participants. When group members are supportive of one another, the group functions well and a positive meeting atmosphere is created. In effective meetings, participants are encouraged to participate in discussion, ask clarifying questions, listen without judgment, share ideas and opinions freely and honestly, and help others from straying from the issue under discussion.[4] Boards of directors can improve the quality of their meetings by applying the following principles:

- Ensure that members understand how their contributions affect both the group and the organization.
- Emphasize the responsibility of each member to the group.
- Establish realistic goals.

- Emphasize pride in belonging to the group.
- Communicate ways to improve the group process.[5]

The following example illustrates how the issue of meeting effectiveness is subject to individual interpretation.

The board of directors of a public agency appointed a task force committee comprised of community residents to assist in developing a long-range plan for the organization. The board provided this citizens group with the following guidelines:

1. Scan elements of the environment that impact the organization (e.g., funding sources, demographics, technology, service needs).
2. Involve the organization's stakeholder (community residents, staff and board) in appropriate ways to achieve maximum input and participation.
3. Maintain regular communications with the board.

At one meeting, the task force committee discussed techniques for gathering stakeholders' ideas and opinions, resulting in a motion *not* to conduct a survey of public opinion. The motion represented a complete departure from one of the committee's primary tasks—to solicit maximum participation from the community in the planning process. Instead, the task force decided to recommend implementation of an ongoing needs assessment in its final report to the organization's board. The vote on the motion was not unanimous; several participants called for clarification. At the end of the meeting some members remained confused about the decision, others were upset with the result of the vote, and still others felt gratified the committee would not divert its planning energies toward assessment activities. (It is important to note that the motion occurred in the last quarter of the meeting and that the decision was made minutes before adjournment. The significance of this timing and the importance of constructing an effective agenda are discussed later in the chapter.)

During the weeks that followed, memos circulated among committee members, the organization's chief executive, and the board chair, and many phone calls were exchanged. Prior to the task force committee's next meeting, an informal consensus developed to revisit the discussion of community participation. At its next meeting, the committee passed a compromise motion outlining a limited number of activities designed to solicit community participation. Resolution of this issue strengthened the committee by providing a sense of achievement and teamwork, as well as dispelling any residual uneasy feelings.

Some board and committee meetings are effective, and some are not; it is unrealistic to expect good meetings 100 percent of the time. Because of differences in participants' expectations, it can be difficult even to agree on what constitutes an effective meeting. An informal poll netted a variety of responses to the question of what characterizes a good meeting.

- "A blend of dedicated people is vital. If [the mix is] right, meetings run smoothly with everyone stepping in to do their part. I would also point to the emotional *connect* with the group. If people feel wanted and appreciated they will go far to help the group." (Past president, John Ball Zoological Society, Grand Rapids, Michigan.)

- "Allow time for sharing of personal stories/successes at the beginning of each meeting." (Jacqueline Haessly, Milwaukee Peace Education Resource Center, Milwaukee, Wisconsin.)

- "At the end of a day you sometimes feel burned out and not in the mood for a meeting. So the things you do to make a meeting more relaxed and more fun, the more creative people are . . . like having food!" (Board member, Arts United of Puget Sound, Seattle, WA.)

- "As the new president of a nonprofit organization, the first thing I did was to stop the previous meeting format in which the executive read to the board from a report they had already received in the mail. If there were questions about a portion of this report that did not require board action, we entertained those questions. Otherwise we discussed only those things that required board action. Also where time limits are set for discussion on a motion, that expedites meetings. . . . A good presiding officer is necessary for an effective meeting." (President of a nonprofit organization, Cape May County, New Jersey.)

- "Good meetings have a purpose and an agenda mailed in advance so our time is spent effectively, and a workable or feasible conclusion is reached." (Officer, Asian Pacific Women's Caucus, Mill Creek, WA.)

- "In the name of efficiency, it is good to come to the board with clear recommendations. But that can sometimes be counterproductive because it doesn't allow for open-ended or probing discussion. If I have to sit and just listen to reports for approval, it's not going to be as much fun." (Board member, Legal Action Center, Chicago, IL.)

These comments not only illustrate that there are many elements of an effective meeting, but also demonstrate a variety of perspectives. The following list summarizes the various aspects of a good meeting.

1. Use participants' valuable time well.
2. Vary the format of meetings, as a strict routine can be dull.
3. Recognize the different needs of meeting participants.
4. Maintain a brisk pace to hold interest.
5. Distribute well-thought-out meeting agendas in advance.
6. Reinforce commitment to the board (and organization) through expressions of appreciation.

SETTING FOCUSED AGENDAS

The board of directors of the Municipal League of King County, WA. effectively uses its organization's planning documents along with carefully developed agendas to guide the board's activities. Members developed a "Decision Flow" to guide board decisions regarding the issues or projects that it will take on. The first question always asked is whether or not an issue is critical to the *survival* of the organization. If it is, then it is placed on the agenda of the organization's annual retreat. All other issues are then passed through a decision tree to determine if they fit the League's mission, balance with other activities, benefit one or more constituent groups, are cost-effective, and so forth. (See "Decision Flow: Municipal League" in Appendix F.) Every January the board, advisers, and staff hold a retreat to discuss and prioritize mission-related issues and problems. Following the retreat, a three year work plan is developed or revised. Because one of the League's primary activities is educating the community about public policy and referendum issues, its work is often driven by the political calendar. To assure a timely response to external events, the League has devised an "Organizational Cycle." This document incorporates the work plan's goals in a month-by-month outline of the organization's major annual activities. (See "Organizational Cycle: Municipal League/Foundation" in Appendix G.) The League's board and committee meetings are very focused because these two organizing documents guide their work. The Decision Flow and Organizational Cycle documents pertain to the League's staff, membership, and two boards, who work together closely to fulfill the organization's mission.[6]

Monthly board meeting agendas are developed by the board chair and president (note: this organization has both a board chair and a board president) based on recommendations from the executive committee, which meets between board meetings. A *timed agenda* is prepared; in such an agenda, each scheduled participant has a designated number of minutes to make his or her presentation. Agenda items are marked as either action items or discussion items so that the board members know in advance which issues require decisions. The agenda and supportive materials are mailed out well in advance of the meeting.

The procedures used by the Municipal League of King Country illustrate an important principle of agenda setting; all matters that are to come before the board or committees should be screened, so that the questions of what shall be discussed and what requires action are resolved before, not during, the meeting. The type of agenda used by the League is much more effective than an open-ended meeting agenda with just three items—old business, new business, other business—which can allow anything (or nothing) to happen.

Before deciding the content of an agenda, three basic questions related to process should be addressed:

1. What category of policy does the issue under consideration address? For example, is the issue one of *ends* or *executive limitations?* (See Carver's governance theory model in Chapter 1 and the discussion of policy setting in Chapter 5.)

2. Who owns the issue? Does it belong to the board or the chief executive? Some organizations share responsibilities between the board and the executive, but shared ownership of an issue area can present a problem. When ownership is unclear or not stated, it is likely to be neglected.

3. What is the board's current position regarding this policy category and how does this new issue relate? The purpose of this question is to determine if the board already has a policy in place that could encompass the new issue. If not, the board must determine whether a more explicit policy, a change in policy, or a different level of policy is needed.[7]

When addressing these questions is consistently made part of the agenda-setting process, a board of directors should be able not only to maintain its focus on policy, but also to understand what needs to be discussed at meetings and what types of decisions need to be made.

Board and committee meeting agenda setting should be a cooperative process between an organization's chief executive and board chairperson or executive committee. Considering the complexity and array of issues today's nonprofit organization executive has to manage, the distinction between management and policy issues can become blurred; it can become difficult to sort out matters that require the board's deliberation. The executive must take responsibility for screening out management issues and bring to the board only those matters pertaining to larger organizational goals. The executive should be prepared to state why an issue should be brought to the board's attention, what the board is expected to do about an issue (set policy, advise, approve), and whether an issue has strategic implications. In other words, "The chief executive provides a structure for the [board] discussions and suggests an appropriate realm for board participation." [8] Since boards are part time and most meet only once a month (at most), issues going to the board need to be prioritized in terms of urgency as well as issue type. Exhibit 7.1 presents a decision tree that can be used by an executive in determining contributions to the board's agenda.

Boards as well as executives must take responsibility for screening management issues from their agendas. A board's chairperson and officers should take the lead in raising questions about the appropriateness of agenda items and speaking out at board meetings to ensure that discussions focus on policy and strategy.

Once the content of agenda items has been determined, they need to be arranged in a logical sequence in order for the meeting to run smoothly. A commonsense approach is the *bell-shaped agenda*. Following the form of a bell-shaped curve, the agenda places easy and noncontroversial items at the beginning and end, with the high points of a meeting (the more difficult agenda items and those requiring action) occurring somewhere in the middle. This structure accommodates latecomers, allows the group time to warm up, and does not stretch the limits of participants' attention spans.[9] The bell-shaped agenda is illustrated in Exhibit 7.2.

PHYSICAL AND PROCEDURAL FACTORS

Although it is common knowledge that physical surroundings contribute to successful meetings, some groups ignore physical factors when arranging a meeting. For example, of all of the rooms available to a community group holding its meetings in a new church facility with spacious community rooms, the meetings (attended by approximately thirty adults) are held in a classroom furnished with child-sized chairs!

Consider also the board of directors of a library that regularly meets in its aging and overcrowded library facility. Because the library has one des-

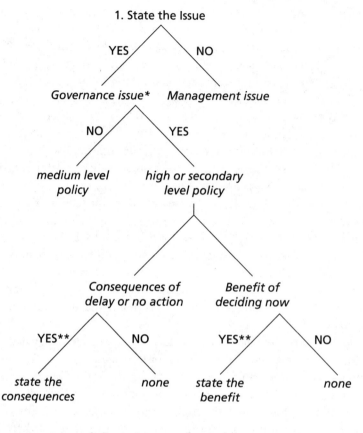

1. State the Issue

YES / NO

Governance issue*   Management issue

NO / YES

medium level   high or secondary
policy   level policy

Consequences of   Benefit of
delay or no action   deciding now

YES** / NO   YES** / NO

state the   none   state the   none
consequences   benefit

2. Repeat process for each issue.

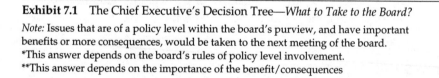

Exhibit 7.1   The Chief Executive's Decision Tree—*What to Take to the Board?*
Note: Issues that are of a policy level within the board's purview, and have important
benefits or more consequences, would be taken to the next meeting of the board.
*This answer depends on the board's rules of policy level involvement.
**This answer depends on the importance of the benefit/consequences

ignated meeting room, which is tiny and uncomfortable, the reference and
periodicals room is used for meetings. This room has a glass wall that looks
out on the main entrance and circulation desk areas, and if patrons need a
periodical they must interrupt the meeting. Both of these physical factors
are distracting.

The effectiveness of meetings can be enhanced by attention to the following physical and procedural factors:

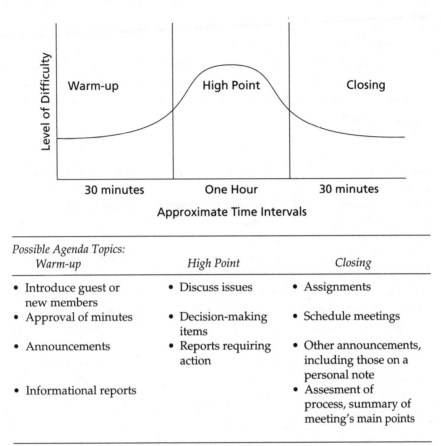

<table>
<tr><td>Level of Difficulty →</td><td>Warm-up</td><td>High Point</td><td>Closing</td></tr>
</table>

30 minutes	One Hour	30 minutes

Approximate Time Intervals

Possible Agenda Topics:

Warm-up	High Point	Closing
• Introduce guest or new members	• Discuss issues	• Assignments
• Approval of minutes	• Decision-making items	• Schedule meetings
• Announcements	• Reports requiring action	• Other announcements, including those on a personal note
• Informational reports		• Assesment of process, summary of meeting's main points

---

Exhibit 7.2   Bell-Shaped Agenda for a Two-Hour Meeting

Source: Adapted from John E. Tropman, "Holding Effective Board Meeting," in *Nonprofit Boards: A Practical Guide to Roles, Responsibilities, and Performance,* by Diane J. Duca (Phoenix: Oryx Press, 1986). Reprinted by permission of Sage Publications.

1. A quiet, light, temperature-controlled room with adequate working space and comfortable chairs is an essential component of a productive meeting. Many organizations feel compelled to conduct board and committee meetings on their premises, regardless of whether the organization's location is accessible and centrally located and whether suitable space is available. It is not necessary to use an organization's facility for meetings if participants can be more comfortable elsewhere.

2. Start on time, and end on time. If meetings consistently begin ten to fifteen minutes late, people will start arriving ten to fifteen minutes

late, resulting in meetings dragging on past their scheduled end, or important agenda items being left unfinished.

3. Adhere to a timed agenda, but maintain flexibility. All participants should share the responsibility for moving business along; peer pressure can be a deterrent to disruptive or distracting behavior from group members.

The chairperson, with support from other members, must ensure that procedures are followed, loose ends are avoided, complex discussions are clarified, and main points are summarized before decisions are made. Officers of a board of directors should be familiar with and follow *Robert's Rules of Order*. The chairperson also is responsible for any necessary follow-up with board or committee members.

Every board should establish its own guidelines for meetings. One option may be to set aside the first board meeting of a new year to evaluate and discuss board procedural issues. Another option may be to discuss board meeting procedures upon the election of a new chairperson. A change in leadership typically brings about a different leadership style, sometimes with different ideas about the management of board and committee meetings. New board members should not have to experience a series of trials and errors before they figure out board meeting protocol and procedures. In setting guidelines for meetings, the following types of questions should be answered:

- How will the board make decisions?
- How will conflicts be resolved?
- To whom are board members accountable for their decisions?
- How will accountability be expressed?
- What procedures will be followed in crisis situations?
- How will annual meetings operate?
- How will regular meetings operate?
- What are the agenda-setting rules?

No group should develop such rigid rules that members have to refer to their manual at every meeting. It is important to acknowledge members' levels of comfort with different meeting styles, and there must be common understanding of procedures if board meetings are to run smoothly and be productive.

MAKING QUALITY DECISIONS

Nonprofit board members anticipate and solve problems for their organization. In order to do this, they should approach problem solving and decision making with both creativity and common sense. It is important to recognize the factors that can limit a board's ability to make quality decisions.

Barriers to Effective Decision Making

A board's effectiveness is reflected in the quality of its decisions. Decisions made in haste or without a reasonable attempt to consider alternatives and different perspectives are typically inferior. The following circumstances contribute to ineffective decision making:

- a full agenda with little time allowed for discussion
- intimidation by the status of certain members
- domination of the group by certain personalities
- suppression of minority viewpoints
- group think
- authoritarian leadership.

The regular occurrence of overly ambitious agendas indicates that either the board is not meeting frequently enough, or the agendas have not been screened carefully. If a board feels pressured to accomplish too much, it is more likely to discuss agenda items in a cursory manner and reach decisions too quickly.

Board members should not defer to other members just because they have power and influence in the community (e.g., elected officials, heads of large companies). Similarly, individuals reluctant to join in discussions because of others' dominant personalities inadvertently limit the alternatives that will be considered. One board chairperson keeps a mental checklist of who has not participated in discussions. "About two-thirds of the way through the meeting, I invite them to comment. This is especially important for engaging new board members who may be hesitant to speak up, and it also works to control any one person from dominating discussions." Chairpersons need to make a conscious effort to draw all members into discussions and ensure that all viewpoints, not just the "popular" ones, are given equal consideration.

Group think occurs when harmony and solidarity are given too much value. Members with different viewpoints are discouraged from expressing them because doing so demonstrates less than total agreement among the members. These conditions inhibit creative problem solving and critical thinking. Harmony should be expressed as congeniality among members, mutual respect, and freedom for members to express themselves. This type of harmony encourages democratic, participatory decision making.

Chairpersons with an authoritarian style can stifle creativity, productivity, and motivation in a board because they tend to come to meetings with predetermined answers rather than with problems for the board to help solve.[10] In contrast, a collaborative style of leadership encourages the communication of different ideas and gives members a sense of ownership in problem solving and decision making for their organization. The increased motivation and commitment on the part of board members are worth the additional time and effort involved in this type of participatory decision making.

Processes for Effective Decision Making

The following elements of effective decision making are essential to the problem solving and policy setting responsibilities of a board of directors:

- *Good communication.* Meetings are a board's primary means of communication and interaction.

- *Separation of perception from fact.* Because board members generally have few opportunities to interact outside the boardroom, it is especially important that they communicate their different perceptions on issues, problems, policies, or proposed solutions. Perceptions need to be separated from facts so that everyone is working toward the same end.

- *The generation of multiple alternatives.* A democratic, collaborative decision-making process is most conducive to unearthing a variety of opinions.

A commonly used collaborative problem-solving method is brainstorming. By way of review, the four basic rules of brainstorming follow:

1. No criticism is allowed. Energies should be directed toward creating ideas, not defending them.

2. There are no limits. Participants are encouraged to communicate whatever comes to mind, since it is easier to modify a far-fetched idea than it is to stretch the parameters of an unimaginative idea.

3. The greater the number of ideas, the more likely it is a solution will result.

4. Participants are encouraged to build on others' ideas by suggesting combinations or alterations. (See "Idea Generating Techniques" in Appendix H.)

A common criticism of brainstorming is that it produces "shallow" or "silly" ideas. However, this only happens if a group does not have sufficient information, if poor judgment is applied when sorting through the options that are generated, or if the process is terminated prematurely, after the first rush of enthusiasm cools.[11]

Jacqueline Haessly, a conflict-resolution specialist, suggests a variation of brainstorming to help groups develop ownership of issues. A larger group can be broken into minigroups and asked to (1) brainstorm perspectives on a problem that needs attention, and (2) think up three or more possible or even improbable solutions. Or, individuals can be asked to write up their own problem lists and solutions; the group's list is then compiled from the individuals' lists. Groups should be encouraged to ask hard questions: Who will benefit from a solution? Who may be excluded or even harmed by the solution? After everyone has had the chance to share their thoughts without comment or criticism from others, the larger group tackles the question of what will work.

The most important decisions an organization must make require extensive participation and involvement.[12] An organization's leaders need to take the responsibility for creating an environment that fosters the development of and nurtures collaboration. Too many leaders rely on structures such as the traditional *consultant-expert* model, where an expert comes in, assesses some problem, and makes specific recommendations on how to fix it. This troubleshooting approach to problem solving assumes every result is traceable to a cause. It is more likely to succeed with simple problems and in situations where cause and effect correspond (e.g., medical emergency response). However, over time, the *process* of working through a problem has been found to be as important as the technical skill and knowledge applied to a problem.[13]

Collaborative decision making works if a leader understands his or her role. According to one school of thought, group facilitators (leaders) are not supposed to participate in the process; their role is to facilitate discussion, support and encourage participation. An alternative view is that leaders should be participants as well as facilitators; they have the same right to express their opinions as the other board members. From this latter perspective, a leader does not always know the right answer but works hard to "create an atmosphere where challenge and pushing one another for better answers becomes the operating style most of the time." [14] This kind of decision-making environment is valuable for the group as well as for leaders because the leaders do not have to bear the burden of coming up with solutions.

Boards and committees may function well in making decisions about routine matters or issues with which they have had some experience, but they may be overwhelmed by crisis situations or external pressure. With a little contingency planning, groups can prepare themselves to manage the unexpected. As stated earlier in this chapter, it is important to have procedures in place for crisis situations. For example, if a board of directors comes under attack from forces external to the organization (e.g., the media, an affiliate organization, clients), the criticism can stimulate useful ideas or prompt thoughtful discussion. Critics also can damage the effectiveness of a board by causing it to lose its objectivity, or causing members to panic and take hasty action just to quiet the criticism. While it should not be used as a substitute for collaborative decision making, expert help may be called for in new situations such as a merger, where the board may not feel competent to assess its options.

Finally, boards of directors should periodically evaluate their decision-making skills. Concluding a meeting by setting aside a time for review is an idea that is growing in popularity. Questions to be addressed might include:

- What was accomplished tonight?
- Did everyone have an opportunity to participate?
- Was the appropriate amount of time given to each agenda item?
- What was not addressed, clarified, or resolved?

SUGGESTIONS FOR FURTHER READING

Blake, Robert R., and James S. Mouton. *Solving Costly Organizational Conflicts: Achieving Intergroup Trust, Cooperation and Teamwork.* San Francisco: Jossey-Bass Publishers, 1984.

Janis, Irving. *Crucial Decisions: Leadership in Policymaking and Crisis Management*. New York: Free Press, 1989.

Peace Talk Publications. Milwaukee Peace Education Resource Center, 2437 No. Grant Blvd., Milwaukee, WI, 53210-2941.

Tropman, John E. *Committee Management in Human Services: Running Effective Meetings, Committees and Boards*, 2nd ed. Chicago: Nelson-Hall, 1992.

Making Meetings Work: Achieving High Quality Group Decisions. Thousand Oaks: Sage Publications, 1995.

CHAPTER EIGHT

Maintaining Focus on Mission

A nonprofit's mission is its reason for being. An effective organization has a clear mission—what the organization does, what it hopes to achieve, who it intends to serve—and communicates this message to the its stakeholders and the public at every possible opportunity. This chapter examines the centrality of an organization's mission and presents evaluation of the program, executive, and board as a means to determine whether an organization is staying on track. A case study of an arts organization illustrates the challenges to their missions that some organizations face.

MISSION AS A BEGINNING

A mission statement defines an organization's value system. Commitment to an organization is, in fact, a reflection of the values shared by its stakeholders.

A mission statement indicates *what* an organization does—what is important, what is valued. It identifies goals or problem areas that the organization intends to address. The mission statement also shows *who* an organization serves, the individuals or groups who are valued. Additionally, the statement may include *how* an organization will conduct its business by identifying the primary method or strategy for meeting its goals (see Exhibit 8.1).

Drafting a mission statement is not easy. Organizers are often so eager to begin a program that their thoughts are focused on activities and methods. It is difficult to step back and consider the underlying meaning of pro-

117

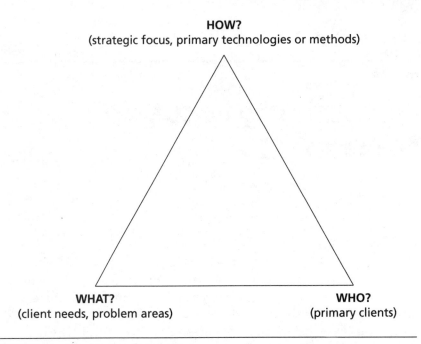

HOW?
(strategic focus, primary technologies or methods)

WHAT?   **WHO?**
(client needs, problem areas)   (primary clients)

Exhibit 8.1   The Mission Statement

gram activities. A good mission statement should be brief yet broad enough to encompass programs conceived for the present and options for the future.

From this statement of purpose and philosophy, the organization's programs and plans are developed. A successful nonprofit uses the mission statement as a guidepost: "It is the starting point. . . . It serves as a criterion for judging the appropriateness of new activities or reevaluating long-standing ones. And it is a rallying point for commitment." [1]

While each organization will have a unique mission statement, the following general guidelines will help focus on the essentials:

1. The mission is more than a statement of good intentions; it must be operational.

2. The mission should accurately state an organization's business. (Peter Drucker once pointed out that hospitals typically state their business as health care. But hospitals do not take care of people's health; they care for the sick and the injured.)

3. Maximum participation in the process of formulating a mission statement helps to ensure ownership and commitment. For a new nonprofit organization, primary stakeholders could be involved in the process of for-

mulating a mission statement rather than a committee of the board. The primary stakeholders of nonprofit organizations are different and must be defined. For a new nonprofit, primary stakeholders may include the steering committee or board of directors; prospective major donors (e.g., United Way, government agencies); potential clients; and major referral sources. The organization's board and staff should be involved in the process of reviewing an existing mission statement.

STAYING ON TRACK

If a nonprofit is to effectively meet its goals, it must continually adjust its programs to changing or new demands, changes in its resources and organizational capacity, and changes in the social, economic, and political environment. Such circumstances may require modifications to the organization's mission. Much as the additions of new programs or adjustments to existing programs must agree with the mission statement, the mission must be adaptable to changing circumstances. An organization that periodically revisits its mission is more likely to remain focused on its primary purpose. Successful organizations maintain an open-minded attitude toward reassessment and reevaluation of their missions.

The Woodland Park Zoo in Seattle, which has won acclaim and exhibit awards from the American Zoo and Aquarium Association, is an example of a successful organization that is working to become even more effective in response to a changing environment. In January 1995, approximately fifty citizens were appointed to a special commission by Seattle's mayor to make recommendations for the zoo's future. The director of the zoo explained that, despite success, it was necessary to plan now for the future in light of several identifiable opportunities and threats. The opportunities were the potential for increasing education and conservation activities. The threats were identified as competition from other important citywide projects (e.g., schools, crime, housing, parks) for city funds to maintain the Zoo's facility (a city asset valued at $500 million) and renovate older exhibits.[2]

Organizations experience crises of mission in different ways. A newly hired executive with a different vision of the organization's future can test the board's commitment to its original mission. A prospective donor may tempt an organization, with the promise of funding, to change the way it does business (e.g., alter its client base or methods of providing service) or take on new programs. In the face of continual funding problems, it is not easy for an organization to decide between alleviating financial insecurity and staying true to its mission. Even nonprofit organizations without financial problems must make hard choices when pressured by some external public to expand into new areas with the temptation of enhanced public recognition.

There is a fine line between effective adaptation within the framework of an organization's mission and unproductive diversion. For example, many Boys Clubs (now Boys and Girls Clubs) began with a mission of recreation and education, but focused primarily on recreational programs. As a holistic approach to social services (addressing a range of individual health, education, and welfare needs rather than one need) gained acceptance in the early 1980s, Boys Clubs shifted their emphasis to broader-based education programs. Recreation is still an important part of the Boys Clubs' tradition, but it is now viewed as a means to enrich the lives of club members rather than as an end in itself.

Zoos are an example of a type of organization with a mission that has evolved dramatically in philosophy and focus. Early zoos had a mission of entertainment; animals were housed in sterile cages and grouped by species to provide the "best views" for visitors. Modern zoos have a mission of public education, conservation of species, and provision of natural habitats.

BENEFITS OF MISSION-FOCUS

A focus on the mission in making decisions will cause a board of directors and executive to address issues relevant to the organization's purpose and values. This focus can be maintained by asking certain questions: Does this issue relate to our mission? How does it impact or advance our mission? These questions must be applied consistently to policy deliberations and decision making regarding programs and clientele, so that the organization stays on track.

A focus on the "big picture" (purpose and values) increases the organization's capacity for strategic response because it forces *forward thinking*, consideration of the future and not just the present situation. A mission-focused organization is in a better position to behave proactively instead of always reacting to problems or crises as they arise. An ability to anticipate the potential impact of changes in the operating environment also can enhance creativity. (See the related discussion on planning strategies in Chapter 5.)

What difference does it make if a nonprofit organization is mission-focused as long as it provides good services? An organization will not be rewarded just because it tries hard and has dedicated people with good intentions. Effective organizations attract the most resources. Numerous studies on what makes a nonprofit organization effective have shown that the primary ingredients of organizational effectiveness are a clear sense of mission and mission-focused governance. These exemplary organizations are said to have integrity. For example, one anonymous donor took the matter of organizational integrity very seriously. In 1995, the Hereditary Disease Foundation of Santa Monica, California, received $500,000 from the estate of an unknown and unsolicited donor. The organization later discovered that the donor had read about the Foundation in a column by Ann Landers in 1983, twelve years before his death: "The Hereditary Disease Foundation . . . spends less than 1 percent of each dollar for promotion, salaries, and office expenses. No other organization comes close. Its integrity is exemplary." [3]

MISSION AS AN END: A CASE STUDY

This is a case of an organization whose mission was put to the test. It ran into serious problems because it paid little attention to its constituents, ignored the dynamics of its external environment, and failed to plan for the future. However, the organization overcame these obstacles, primarily because its board of trustees was willing to stay the course during a long period of transition.

The Corporate Council for the Arts (CCA) in Seattle, Washington, was founded in 1969 (as the United Arts Fund) by a group of community business leaders who wanted an efficient way for corporations to contribute to the growing number of arts organizations in the Puget Sound region. Their mission was "to serve the business community by acting as its instrument for raising and distributing unrestricted operating funds on an annual basis for qualifying arts organizations." Secondarily, the fund was to provide a stable source of funding for its beneficiary arts organizations. Modeled after other united funds, the CCA was founded on two basic principles: (1) protection of contributors from a barrage of fund-raising appeals by providing an efficient, forum for making contributions; and (2) offering beneficiary agencies a reliable source of annual funds while saving them the time and expense of conducting separate fund drives.

This narrow interpretation of the purpose of a united fund for the arts seemed to suffice for nearly ten years. But two significant changes within CCA's primary constituent groups threatened the organization. First, corporations were becoming more professional in their approach to grant making; many had hired contributions officers who were highly knowledgeable about community resources, evaluating appeals, and grant-making processes. Second, arts organizations also were becoming more professional, and their financial needs were growing rapidly. The CCA neither kept pace with its agencies' growth by raising more funds nor involved itself in policy issues about public funding of the arts and capital campaigns.

By 1985, CCA's problems came to a head. Arts agencies were bypassing them by raising large sums of money directly from corporations; CCA was not only falling short in fulfilling its mission, but it was also being challenged by charges that its distribution system was inequitable. In 1986 and 1987, the board issued new guidelines for distribution of funds and convened a meeting of about one hundred contributors and beneficiaries to present its new plan. For the first time, both constituencies of the CCA were together in the same room. But when it was revealed that funds given directly by a corporation to an arts organization would be deducted from the recipient's CCA allocation, the proceedings came to a standstill.

Following that unproductive meeting, the board questioned the viability of the organization. Did the organization still serve a purpose? Should it continue? How should it handle the problems it was experiencing? Adding to the difficulties, the organization's problems were widely known because of extensive press coverage. A mandate for change was clear.

The board formed a Role Committee to reexamine the mission of CCA. The committee was asked to address three broad topics:

1. the role of CCA in relation to the business and arts communities
2. the criteria to be used in making grants
3. a regional approach to CCA's annual fund drive.

According to a new modus operandi outlined in the committee's report to the board, CCA should:

- Develop a justifiable case for increased support of the arts.
- Set realistic campaign goals based on the assessed needs of arts agencies.
- Recognize the role of corporate grant makers and include them in the process.
- Poll corporate members to determine if insulation from solicitation by individual organizations is desired.

- Establish higher minimum levels of giving.
- Educate the public and arts organizations about the extent to which businesses contribute to the arts.
- Provide fiscal oversight to beneficiary agencies.
- Retain a regional focus.[4]

Additionally, the committee revised eligibility and review criteria. The board adopted the committee's report in 1989 and began a search for a new executive to implement its directives.

Today, CCA's mission remains the same, but the way it operates has changed dramatically. Over the five-year period between 1989 and 1994, the CCA increased its grant funds by 50 percent. The number of arts organizations receiving grants grew from twenty-three to fifty-three. Its grant making has evolved from a casual and haphazard process (called "appalling" by one board member), to a systematic review process that allows beneficiaries and prospective recipients to make presentations before the Allocations Committee. During the last three years, CCA also has ventured into workplace giving in about twenty companies. The organization and its donors receive more recognition for their accomplishments than in the past, and the CCA is taking a proactive stance in pursuing new and innovative opportunities to advance the arts in the Puget Sound region.

The CCA still has much to do. Its achievements in recent years and its turnaround can be attributed to the commitment of the board of trustees. What made the difference, even when the organization was floundering and on the brink of extinction, was that board members stayed around to see that change was implemented.[5]

EVALUATION AND ASSESSMENT

How does a nonprofit organization know if it is true to its mission and staying on track? A good mission statement emphasizes achievement. But an organization cannot know if it is actually achieving results unless time is devoted to monitoring overall performance.

A Board's Role in Evaluation

Evaluation is a critical activity that is too often avoided by a nonprofit board of directors. Board members need not question every detail of an organization's operations, but the complacent board that fails to question the rationale behind major decisions could endanger the overall health of the organization. A board participates in setting an organization's goals, and must ensure their implementation.

Effective oversight requires information. There are literally hundreds of questions to ask about an organization's programs, finances, community relationships, and so forth. Many resources on the subject of program evaluation as well as self-assessments specifically designed for nonprofits are available through university and public libraries. (See also "Suggestions for Further Reading" at the end of this chapter.) The following are some strategic, mission-related questions that board members should ask:

- What is the purpose of X program?
- What results are expected from the program?
- What problem areas not presently served by the program need attention?
- Who does the organization want to serve tomorrow?
- How do clients benefit from the organization's services?
- What does the organization offer that others do not?
- Where is the organization succeeding? In which areas is it less than successful?
- If the organization ceased to exist, would it be missed?

The actual conduct of an evaluation is the staff's responsibility, although some boards prefer to conduct an informal review. Generally, a board of directors asks questions about progress toward policy ends, and the staff provides evidence. Then, the board decides whether or not progress toward those ends is sufficient to merit the continued application of resources. A sample evaluation process follows:

1. A family services organization has a policy stating that it will give highest priority to assisting children among the homeless, from welfare households, and in other of the poorest populations.
2. The board asks if the policy is being followed and with what success.
3. The staff provides data on the number and type of service hours devoted to the targeted children's populations, compared to the total clients served, plus financial documentation to demonstrate whether or not the program is cost-effective.

A board also needs to ensure that there are policies to guide evaluation processes. First a board must know what it wants the organization to accomplish, then it can develop a policy on evaluation that emphasizes those goals. When a board evaluates the entire organization, the mission is the standard against which all performance is measured. When program effectiveness is being evaluated, program goals and objectives are the performance standards.

Approaching Evaluation

The results of an evaluation provide board members with information that can diminish uncertainties about their organization's operations, help to clarify the value of their decisions, or signal a warning if the organization is not operating according to its mission. Boards must be sensitive to the issues surrounding social services program evaluation so that they can frame questions appropriately and avoid unrealistic demands on staff. The following is a list of characteristics of nonprofits that can help board members to understand the complexity of nonprofit organization evaluation.

1. *Multiple performance criteria.* Nonprofit social services organizations rarely have a measure of profitability and often have multiple program goals and objectives. This makes it very difficult to identify any one or two performance measures that can be applied across a variety of programs.

2. *Lack of comparability.* The performance of two nonprofit museums may be compared, but it is impossible to compare the effectiveness of a museum with that of a hospital. This presents a major problem in the allocation of funds among public services. How can resources be allocated fairly if the effectiveness of different organizations cannot be compared?

3. *Nonfinancial performance measures.* Since the mission of most nonprofit organizations is service, measures of effectiveness are not based on financial statements, but on client satisfaction, client response to treatment, impact on clients' quality of life, or other qualitative indicators.

4. *Indirect relationship between costs and benefits.* The relationship between input and output in a nonprofit cannot be accurately measured. Would adding another professional social worker benefit the community by an amount that exceeds the added cost to an organization? How much money should be spent on trying to find a cure for chil-

dren's diabetes? While these types of questions are difficult to analyze in quantitative terms, the issue of value should not be ignored.

5. *Staff limitations.* Evaluation activities should not take precedence over
an organization's programs. Conflicting demands on staff time presents a dilemma in conducting thorough and systematic evaluations.

Organizations can become preoccupied with processes of evaluation
and appropriate measures of program performance. For fear of not being
able to conduct a proper evaluation, some organizations resist evaluation
altogether. As difficult as the task may be, a nonprofit must make some effort to assess how well it is doing.

Within any organization there are likely to be different opinions about
what an evaluation should accomplish. Board members may expect to gain
insight on the impact of programs over the long term, while the chief executive may be more concerned with current administrative issues and
client satisfaction, and program staff may want to learn which methods of
service delivery are working as planned. These different expectations must
be sorted out in advance in order to achieve the best results.

An organization should be prepared to deal with unexpected findings.
For example, a library commissioned a survey and found, to its surprise,
that among those who did not use the library, there was a high percentage
who felt they could not afford it. Some community residents were unaware
that the public library was free. The proper response to such a result would
be to create a different approach to marketing of services.

Expectations about program outcomes need to be considered in a different cultural context when nonprofit organizations with international
programs undergo evaluation. Because values differ from culture to culture, and because measures of program success and organizational effectiveness are based upon those values, various cultures define success differently. The boards of international organizations have dual
responsibilities in their evaluation oversight role. They must be sensitive
to the characteristics of their home-based organizations that relate to evaluations (e.g., those outlined above), and to the culture-specific issues of their
programs overseas.

The criteria for evaluation are different for nonprofit organizations in
other countries (called nongovernmental organizations, NGOs), especially
for those active in Third World or developing nations in Asia, Africa, and
Latin America. These NGOs' are faced with the challenging goals of empowerment and economic development, and effective performance focuses
on:

1. An NGO's ability to involve indigenous village and neighborhood groups in processes to help them become "protagonists or subjects of their own and society's development."

2. Social and economic development that does not compromise the resources of future generations.[6]

While Third World professionals prefer to emphasize social indicators of empowerment when describing a program's achievements, funding sources in Western industrialized nations that provide assistance to Third World organizations stress the use of tangible economic indicators as measures of program success. These opposing viewpoints suggest that the social and economic goals of NGOs should be evaluated separately. Because the majority of NGOs do not document their accomplishments, the debate over what program goals to measure or what methodologies to apply is as yet unresolved.[7]

Nonetheless, within the last five years there has been increasing recognition by NGOs of the need to develop measures that can express program results in both social and economic terms. The following examples illustrate how success in economic terms is linked to social factors.

- In Costa Rica, an NGO housing program built thirteen hundred homes at a significantly lower cost compared to homes built by the government or the private sector. Cost-effectiveness was attributed to the organization's use of "trained self-help," ordinary people who were involved in all aspects of the construction projects.[8]

- In Honduras, a water system developed by an NGO was technically successful and very cost-effective. But, as one observer put it, the group's real success was not so much the technical factor associated with the project, but the human factors, such as the cooperation that occurred to solve a major problem in a village. What made *Agua para el Pueblo* unusual was "their view that water [projects] can be used to raise community consciousness." [9]

Assessing the Executive's Performance

A board of directors must have a clear understanding of its role and the role of the organization's chief executive in order to judge the performance of the executive fairly. A board should monitor whether or not its executive is making expected progress toward achieving the outcomes stated in policies, and ensuring that the executive does not violate whatever limitations the board has placed on his or her position (e.g., standards or ethics, rules on diligence, expenditures).

Many nonprofit boards do not realize that when they ask their executives questions about program progress and outcomes, they are actually monitoring executive performance. Instead, they consider the performance appraisal as the one occasion set aside annually when the executive and board of directors formally discuss the executive's work and when comments are put in writing. A good and fair assessment of the executive involves both the informal monitoring and a more formal annual appraisal, and engages the full board of directors.

Often, a nonprofit board's personnel committee or an ad hoc committee evaluates an executive, and the full board ratifies the committee's report. When a board charges a committee with evaluating the executive, it is abdicating what should be a collective responsibility. The problem with a committee approach is that a small group of individuals may discuss executive performance based on their personal expectations and perspectives, tally "yes" and "no" responses, and present the result as if it were an official board response. Committee bias can be diminished somewhat by making sure that there are preestablished criteria for evaluation, but *full* board participation is the preferred method of assessment. It is reasonable to expect a board with up to thirty-five members to act as a committee of the whole in the matter of executive evaluation. Larger boards may be forced to use a different process to gather opinions from the full board about their executive's performance, such as a survey questionnaire.

In exercising its responsibility for executive performance evaluation, a nonprofit board of directors should follow these general guidelines:

- Define the purpose of the formal evaluation. It should be based on a desire to improve an executive's performance, recognize accomplishments, and encourage personal growth on the job. It must be constructive.

- Review the executive's job description. A job description can become outdated, especially when an executive has been with the organization for many years. The position description may include responsibilities that have since been delegated to other staff positions, or it may inappropriately credit certain responsibilities to the executive that are in fact within the board's purview.

- Share every aspect of the evaluation process with the executive to demonstrate accountability.

- Perform evaluations as frequently as practicable. If evaluation of the executive is limited to once a year or less frequent intervals, there is a greater risk that the appraisal may be neither accurate nor fair. Psychological studies have shown that individuals tend to have a sharp recall of recent or dramatic events but only a limited recollection of distant or ordinary ones. For example, if an executive were to become involved in a conflict with the board a month before evaluation, could the board overlook the incident and give due credit for the executive's accomplishments prior to the conflict? Conversely, if a major grant based on the executive's proposal is awarded to the organization shortly before evaluation, but over the past year the executive has been a rather mediocre performer, how might the board's judgment be influenced?

- Outline the criteria for evaluation in the letter of agreement if an executive has been hired on a contractual basis. The board should ensure that the evaluation follows the prescribed performance standards.

- Relate the executive's performance to the advancement of the organization's goals.

- Establish a time frame for any necessary changes. Any plan for improvement must be mutually agreed upon by the executive and the board.

A Board's Self-Assessment

Just as nonprofit boards assume oversight responsibility for their organizations and evaluate their executives, they also need to take their own pulse from time to time. The challenges facing nonprofit boards today require imaginative leadership and the ability to thoughtfully examine basic organizational issues such as quality and costs. A board needs to periodically assess its leadership capacity in order to ensure that the organization is served well. An assessment that helps bring about positive and practical changes in the board as a group and in members' performance is a worthwhile investment of the board's time.

Principles of Self-Assessment. A number of principles of self-assessment apply equally to organizations and individuals:

1. Public rather than confidential assessments are most likely to produce change. Because an initial step in any change process is to identify

Note: This is just a *sampling* of process, procedure, content, and focus questions a board might want to ask itself. It is not intended to be a complete checklist, and the questions do not appear in any particular order.

1. Do board members have job descriptions?
   yes_____   no_____
2. Are prospective board members told that they may be expected to:

make a personal contribution	yes_____	no_____	unknown_____
ask others for money	yes_____	no_____	unknown_____
serve on a fund-raising committee	yes_____	no_____	unknown_____
sell tickets to a fund-raising event	yes_____	no_____	unknown_____

3. Which of the following statements best describe board meetings? Check all that apply.
   fun_____; interesting_____; boring_____
   too long_____; about the right length_____; too short_____
   move briskly_____; move at a snail's pace_____
   most members participate in discussions_____; a few members tend to dominate discussions_____
   members feel free to express ideas and opinions_____; members are reluctant to speak up_____
4. At the last two board meetings, how many times did someone raise a question about the relevance of an issue to the organization's mission?
   never_____; once or twice_____; often_____
5. If a staff member other than the executive comes to you with a complaint, do you know what to do?
   yes_____   no_____
6. Which of the following statements best describe the communications the board receives from the chief executive? Check all that apply.
   too much information_____; just the right amount of information_____; too little information_____
   sometimes information is irrelevant_____; communications are unclear and without direction_____; communications are mixed_____; the executive prefaces communications with a statement regarding its purpose_____
7. Which of these characteristics apply to the majority of board members? Check all that apply.
   zealously committed to the organization's mission_____; loyal to the organization and its cause_____; strong interest in board activities_____; probably concerned about the organization and its mission but not overtly expressed_____; uneven display of interest in board activities_____
8. Which of the following statements best describe board committee activity? Check all that apply.
   members serve on two or more committees_____; members serve on one committee_____
   members choose the committee on which they will serve_____; members are assigned to committees_____

there are too many committees_____ ; there are just the right number of com-
mittees_____ ; more committees are needed_____
committees don't do much_____ ; committees do too much_____
9. The board has an annual work plan that outlines what it intends to accomplish over the next year, the decisions it needs to make, and a time frame.
yes_____   no_____   unknown_____
10. Are minutes of the last meeting and an agenda for upcoming meetings sent
out in advance?
yes_____   no_____   sometimes_____
11. Are board members generally knowledgeable about the community, particularly changes in the social, economic, and political environment that may impact the organization?
yes_____   no_____
12. Which of the following statements best describes the *climate* of the board?
Pick one.
cool_____ ; stormy_____ ; foggy_____ ; hot_____ ; cloudy with occasional
showers_____ ; clear and bright_____ ; fresh breezes_____ ; other_____

Follow-up instructions: Discuss the responses to each question and determine
whether no improvement is needed, a minor adjustment/improvement is
needed, or some major change is required. After determining the necessary
changes, establish a time frame for accomplishing them.

Exhibit 8.2   Nonprofit Board Self-Assessment Questions

Adapted from: Nancy S. Nordhoff, Jo Larsen, Putnam Barber, and Dorothy P. Craig,
*Fundamental Practices for Success with Volunteer Boards of Nonprofit Organizations: A Self-
Assessment & Planning Guide,* (Seattle: FunPrax Associates, 1982), 95.

where you are at the present and where you would like to be, self-
assessment includes a description of the present and a prescription
for the future. The opportunity to share in the ownership of change
enables change to occur with less trauma.

2. Assessment involves gathering data about what is happening and
what should be happening in the organization, and individuals' perceptions about these facts. It is a process of determining truths about
the organization and its members and making those truths public
within the organization.

3. A good self-assessment leads to action. A main goal of personal and
organizational assessment is to enhance individuals' capacity to dis-
cern truths and act on them.

4. Self-assessments are highly subjective and unique to a particular organization. The concept of effectiveness is a social judgment affected

by individual perceptions. The growing body of literature on nonprofit boards focuses on characteristics of high-performing, effective boards. However, the value of a board's self-assessment lies in the insights it offers regarding different board members' perspectives on a variety of issues, not in comparisons with other organizations. Self-assessment can disclose areas of consensus or disagreement, and, depending on the questions asked, it can suggest direction, point up weaknesses that require attention, or disclose previously unknown strengths.

How Are We Doing? Preparing for an assessment is an essential part of the assessment process. Board members need to decide if they want to assess board practices and procedures, themselves, or both. They also should determine the following:

- What type of evaluation is most likely to elicit information relevant to the governance role?
- What specific information is needed?
- How will the results be used?
- Should an outside facilitator be consulted?

Once these questions have been addressed, an ad hoc board committee could collect and review different self-assessment tools for finding a set of questions that can elicit the information a board requires. Exhibit 8.2 illustrates one such set of questions. Local United Ways or many national organizations can provide their affiliated organizations with assessment tools and checklists.

SUGGESTIONS FOR FURTHER READING

Bennis, Warren. *On Becoming a Leader*. Reading: Addison-Wesley Publishing, 1989.

Drucker, Peter F. *The Five Most Important Questions You Will Ever Ask About Your Nonprofit Organization*. San Francisco: Jossey-Bass Publishers, 1993. (A self-assessment tool.)

Field Guide to Outcome-Based Program Evaluation. Booklet available from: Evaluation Forum, 811 First Ave., Suite 200; Seattle, Wash., 98104.

Graham, John W., and Wendy C. Haulick. *Mission Statements: A Guide to the Corporate and Nonprofit Sectors*. New York: Garland, 1994.

Pierson, Jane, and Joshua Minta. "Assessment of the Chief Executive: A Tool for Governing Boards and Chief Executives of Nonprofit Organizations." Washington, D.C.: National Center for Nonprofit Boards, 1995.

Slesinger, Larry H. *Self-Assessment for Nonprofit Governing Boards.* Washington, D.C.: National Center for Nonprofit Boards, 1995 rev. ed.

Wong-Rieger, Durhane, and Lindee David. "A Hands-On Guide to Planning and Evaluation," 1993. Available through: National Aids Clearinghouse, 1565 Carling Ave., Suite 40; Ottawa, Ontario K1Z 8R1, Canada.

CHAPTER NINE

New Challenges for Nonprofit Boards

The nonprofit sector makes significant economic, social, and democratic contributions to society. Yet despite their value, nonprofit organizations must continually justify their existence. At the fall 1995 meeting of the Independent Sector, nonprofits were criticized for being too insular; the public is not generally aware of what they do. According to leaders in the nonprofit sector, such as John Gardner and Lester Salamon, nonprofits need to improve their public image—and the time to do that is now.

The climate in which all contemporary organizations operate is changing at a faster pace than ever before. Unfortunately, many nonprofits are slow to respond to their environment, and some continue to operate in a state of blissful ignorance about what is happening outside their own organizations. The purpose of this final chapter is to describe some of the significant issues and challenges facing nonprofits. A case study of a women's organization illustrates how some nonprofit organizations have learned to adapt in response to these challenges.

GOVERNMENT RELATIONS

Management of relationships with the various levels of government is estimated to account for one-third of the expenditures of nonprofit service providers (e.g., health care, education, social welfare).[1] The government affects the operating environment of the nonprofit sector in several ways:

1. The government is a funding source and partner in service delivery.

2. The government supports the nonprofit sector through tax breaks, special mail rates, and tax deductions for donors.

3. The government regulates the nonprofit sector through the Internal Revenue Service, charitable solicitation laws, nonprofit incorporation procedures, and other regulatory standards for certain subsectors (e.g., housing, health care).

4. Nonprofits are involved in attempting to change government policy through lobbying activities, voter and referendum education, and advocacy for groups with special needs.

With some exceptions, boards are predominantly involved in the service contracting area of government-nonprofit relations. It is critical for the boards of nonprofits receiving government funds to understand the changing context of government-nonprofit contracting relationships and how that impacts their organizations. "The changing nature of service delivery and the methods of funding services have caused the change from a collaborative model between nonprofit and government to a competitive model between all three [nonprofit, government, business] sectors." [2] According to The Union Institute's Office of Social Responsibility, in Washington D.C., this perceived loss of collaboration and subsequent competition between the government, business, and nonprofit sectors has undermined the public's regard for nonprofit organizations. A senior economic development analyst with the city of Seattle attributes this to a general cynicism toward government and public scrutiny of government activities, both of which have had repercussions for nonprofits in the following ways:

1. An increasing number of government services are being privatized, which means more contracting out to nonprofits (and for-profits). There is a widespread perception that the private sector (business or nonprofit) can provide services more efficiently and effectively than the government and that privatization allows citizens to have a greater voice in selecting among public goods and services. Confidence in the government's ability to effectively manage its affairs has been seriously eroded with tales of fraud, waste, and abuse. The distrust of government agencies as service providers has unfortunately been transferred to the new service providers.

2. Increased public scrutiny of public expenditures has led government agencies to enact stricter auditing requirements in their service con-

tracts. This results in an added expense for nonprofits without internal accounting staff to conduct contract audits.

The trend in government funding toward more narrowly defined service areas and eligibility criteria is perceived by nonprofit contractees as a threat to their autonomy. For example, government grantors may request a nonprofit to expand its service areas, client base, or even type of services as a condition of the contract. A nonprofit engaging in its first government contract can choose to reject the contract, but for a group renewing its service contract, such demands may challenge its mission. The nonprofit may have developed a dependence on government funds that would make it much more difficult to terminate the contract relationship.

According to some critics, the changing nature of government-nonprofit contracting has forced nonprofit boards of directors to become more political.[3] A recent study of four hundred nonprofit organizations examined the influence of nonprofit boards on the government-nonprofit relationship. It was found that boards are not passive bystanders, but take on the various roles of facilitator, political advocate, buffer, or values guardian.[4]

A board that functions as a *facilitator* may assist in the preparation of grants, attend meetings with government granting agencies as part of a strategy to demonstrate the board's support of the organization's programs, promote or participate in community networking, review and approve government contracts, and ask probing questions regarding contract arrangements.

Board members who engage in specific activities, such as writing or calling legislators to urge support on an issue critical to their organization, its field, or the nonprofit sector in general, function as *political advocates*. They may actively campaign for referendums related to their cause and to the nonprofit sector in general.

A board that functions as a *buffer* between the government and nonprofit sector may work to protect a nonprofit from overregulation or loss of autonomy in a contracting relationship, analyze options for government contracting by examining the relationship between the government's goals and the organization's mission, and monitor other activities.

Lastly, the role of a board as *values guardian* is based on the notion that board service is an opportunity for citizen participation. "In this role, the board acts against the potentially undermining effect of state contracts by articulating nonprofit organizational values, mission, and self-set priorities. Meeting community need is emphasized as a central responsibility of the board."[5]

The following variables influence the role that a nonprofit board adopts with respect to government relations:

- the proportion of government funds to other sources of revenue
- the size and age of an organization
- the degree to which an executive educates the board of directors about government contracting
- affiliation with other associations, collaboration or networking in the community
- degree of professionalism among staff.

Nonprofit boards that have adopted policies promoting stakeholder relationships are more likely to assume a proactive role in government relations than boards not engaged in external relations. In summary, boards serve to balance the interdependent relationship between the government and nonprofit sectors of society.

THE IMPACT OF PROFESSIONALISM

Nonprofit organizations are becoming more professional in response to stricter government regulations that require compliance with certain standards, and growing public expectations for quality services provided by trained personnel. Several years ago, the president of the National Easter Seal Society reflected that commitment will no longer run an organization: "You also have to have professionalism or you're going to go out of business." Professionalism in the nonprofit sector refers to the growing number of chief executives and staff with specialized training in their service areas, including advanced degrees and specific managerial competencies. In many cases the trend toward professionally oriented staff has created tension and conflict between the board and the staff.

Each type of professional produces a different potential area of conflict between the board and staff.[6] Consider the different perspectives professionals from various fields bring to their work in a nonprofit organization, and the types of questions they are likely to raise:

1. Professional management staff (e.g., those with master's degrees in business, certified public accountants, marketing experts) may challenge the primacy of the role the board plays in planning and policy

setting on the basis that they (the staff) are better qualified. In particular, staff may question the appropriateness of placing fiduciary responsibilities in the hands of a volunteer board whose members are not management professionals.

2. Professional staff with expertise, training, and credentials specific to a field of interest (e.g., museum curators, scientists, psychologists, health-care professionals) may be more focused on services and programs and dismiss matters of efficiency and effectiveness that concern the board. Professional training has given these staff a "tenacious attachment to what they know—they are less likely to want to put on the corporate hat or even to look at the interests of the community that they serve, or set aside personal interests than their predecessors might have been." [7]

3. Academically oriented staff (e.g., those with doctorates in public administration, education, sociology) have acquired more than knowledge of a discipline and the mastery of special skills, they have been socialized into their profession, with its attendant norms, values, and role models. These professionals may feel a division of loyalties between the standards of their profession and their organization, which can create ethical conflict. Lay board members may be unaware of the various professional standards and norms, or of where staff loyalties lie.

CHANGING ROLE OF THE EXECUTIVE

The complex environment in which nonprofits currently operate demands different sets of executive skills and competencies than were required ten or fifteen years ago. The role of a nonprofit executive has expanded beyond managing an organization's internal affairs to include the critical function of *boundary-spanning:* a contemporary nonprofit executive must know how to interact effectively with the organization's external environment—to broker opportunities, to create and sustain networks, to position the organization to adapt to changes in the resource environment, to monitor and analyze the needs and demands of stakeholders, and so forth. But the executive also must be skilled in managing the organization's internal environment, as human resource developer, strategic planner, and overseer of program services.[8]

The position description of the chief executive of the Northwest Network for Youth captures the complex nature of the role of today's nonprofit administrator by defining the executive's responsibilities in three broad categories: relationships with the board, organizational management and leadership, and building community awareness. The following statements of responsibilities are a sampling from the Network's position specification, which appears in full in Appendix I:

- Promote a greater exchange of information between and with youth serving agencies, locally, regionally and nationally.
- Facilitate annual Board retreat to include a strategic planning process in order to accomplish short and long term goals and objectives.
- Work with the Board to implement a long-term vision and organizational plan and to enhance the diversity of the Network on an ongoing basis.
- Position the Network to be the leading trainer for youth workers in Region X.
- Quickly become a visible and persuasive facilitator of youth and family issues.

In order to accommodate this shift of executive energy toward an organization's external environment, a board first needs to empower its executive to fulfill his or her boundary-spanning functions by establishing policies that promote external relations and community networking. Second, board members must adjust their executive recruitment and hiring practices. The executive's job description as well as the criteria for evaluation may need to be revised.

COLLABORATION AND STRATEGIC ALLIANCES

Nonprofit organizations in all fields are aggressively pursuing partnerships and alliances, transforming the way they do business. Collaboration has become the norm because funds are limited, many community and human services are duplicative or overlapping (e.g., one province in Canada reports thirty-seven AIDS organizations), and private and public funders encourage strategic alliances. Most requests for proposals now ask how the applicant plans to cooperate with other agencies in the community. Planned collaboration strengthens an applicant's request for support.

The most common form of collaboration is facility sharing. Buildings are expensive to maintain and it makes sense to share the overhead whenever possible. For example, a community center in Denver, Colorado, shares its facility with a day care center and the offices of a Kiwanis camp, and sublets space to a public school's tutorial program. A strategic variation of this model is exemplified by a joint venture undertaken by three nonprofits that created a "one-stop services center" in their community. A new shopping strip was unable to attract retail tenants and remained vacant for a number of years. A consortium of nonprofit organizations approached the owners, who agreed to sell the property at a reduced price. Within two years, the strip mall was fully occupied by ten nonprofits and two other businesses. The three nonprofits involved in the initial planning purchased the property jointly through a separate legal partnership, and tenants pay rent to the partnership.

Other nonprofits have found that purchasing or leasing space of their own is no longer essential to their operations. Many organizations are turning to more flexible and mobile program delivery models (e.g., outreach programs, extension programs at multiple sites) rather than anchoring themselves to one facility in one location. This is an increasingly important alternative for urban agencies given that neighborhoods change rapidly and organizations may find themselves without clientele.

The board of directors is responsible for major decisions about a nonprofit's facility or alternative arrangements to accommodate the organization's programs. There are several questions a board should ask when considering sharing a facility.

- Will the organization be able to maintain its identity, especially if it is one of the smaller agencies involved?
- If the anchor agency pulls out of a common facility, how will that impact the others involved?
- How will common facilities help to foster integrated services for clientele?
- Will a common facility diminish accessibility by reducing the number of locations at which community and human services are offered?

Nonprofit organizations also are collaborating in planning and conducting community needs assessments and feasibility studies. Because one organization often lacks the resources to conduct an in-depth community or customer-related analysis, pooling resources enables the participating nonprofits to acquire valuable strategic information unavailable to them individually.

For example, the board of directors of a large countywide Planned Parenthood organized a task force of board members to study the issues of reform and fee structure. Planned Parenthood organizations are being forced to reexamine the entire premise of their operations in response to national health care reform and state initiatives on managed health care. Planned Parenthood needs to demonstrate that it is an essential community provider in order to survive in the new health care management environment.

Members of the task force recognized that these issues were too complex for them to assess on their own. They joined with the boards from other Planned Parenthood affiliates in the state to conduct an in-depth feasibility study and analyze their options. The chief executive of one Planned Parenthood said this was the first time the affiliates had collaborated:

> Previously, each organization had the attitude that they were so unique, despite a common mission, that there was no basis for cooperation. The changing environment forced us to focus on a common problem and created a new willingness to share. The evolution of health care is proving to be an interesting problem for the boards. They're having to take an entrepreneurial approach and consider new ways for billing state health providers, and they have become advocates for Planned Parenthood's mission and clients.[9]

Other collaborative endeavors revolve around fund-raising. In any community, fund-raising events by different organizations compete for many of the same patrons' time and money. It is often difficult for nonprofits to enlist sufficient volunteers, gain media attention and publicity. In collaborative fundraising, two or more agencies may join forces to put on a fund-raising event (e.g., auction, dinner, street fair, concert) and share the proceeds. If the cooperating organizations all provide services to children and youth, for example, patrons do not have to choose which organization's events to support. They may be more willing to pay $500 to attend a single function than attend two or three events at $150 each.

Collaboration represents a fundamental shift in the ways in which staff, volunteers, and board members have worked in the past. For years, nonprofits were taught (at seminars, through fund-raising literature) that in order to attract resources, they needed to sell themselves as unique and focus on how they were different from other organizations in the community or in their field. What may have begun as a marketing and fund-raising pitch, over time became part of organizations' belief systems. Too many nonprofit have the attitude that their organization's services are so unique that there could not possibly be common grounds for cooperating with another organization. This parochial perspective has prevented many nonprofits from exploring options for collaboration.

When collaboration represents substantive change for an organization, the chief executive and the board must be fully supportive in order to legitimize the proposed endeavor. The board also must be alert to the potential impact of collaboration on an organization's mission and whether or not policy adjustments are necessary.

The Trend Toward Mergers

The ultimate form of collaboration is a merger. It sometimes evolves from a long-term collaboration between two agencies that come to recognize not only the complementary nature of their programs, but also the potential for greater accomplishments as one united organization. A merger also can occur for reasons of survival, greater efficiency in operations, or growth. It is a strategic option for fulfilling an organization's mission or achieving major goals such as improved client services or economies of scale. However, the primary catalyst for a merger between two nonprofit organizations is economic uncertainty.[10]

A merger is neither appropriate for every organization nor the best solution to an organization's problems. Ideally, a merger would join two healthy nonprofits. If two organizations with serious problems merge, their difficulties may only be magnified. A nonprofit's leadership should consider merging as an option when planning the organization's future. Whether or not a merger is a serious possibility, the board and executive can benefit from a discussion of the advantages and disadvantages of such a union.

The advantages of merging include:

- enhanced financial and technological synergy
- the opportunity to expand services
- an expanded donor base
- access to new expertise and additional resources
- cost savings on administrative expenditures
- opportunity for staff development and career advancement
- improved efficiency by reduction in overlap of services
- greater market recognition.

Some of the disadvantages of merging are:

- difficulties in redesigning programs
- potential loss of identity
- difficulties in redefining staff responsibilities
- potential for clash of organizational cultures
- incompatibility of staffs
- conflicts of power.

Merging the boards of directors of two nonprofits presents a different set of issues, with a variety of options in terms of board size and structure. One board could cease to exist or two boards could combine to create one larger board. If the size of the combined board is too large, there are additional options:

1. There are usually some board members more interested in program activities than policy setting, planning, or monitoring fiscal affairs; so, an alternative is to offer those members the option of serving on a program advisory committee or auxiliary body.
2. Planning a merger and overseeing its implementation require additional time and energy from a board. Once the merger is complete, there may be those who desire a less time-consuming option than serving on the corporate board of directors. These individuals also may be candidates for serving on an advisory or auxiliary body.
3. There may be some board members who feel very strongly linked to the original organization and elect to resign.

Other aspects of merging two boards of directors are more difficult to manage. Boards should be aware that the following intangible factors also pose a challenge to a smooth merger:

- establishment of commitment to the new organization
- motivation of board members to stay with the new organization until it is running smoothly
- creation of a new board culture
- replacement of old, comfortable associations with new relationships.

A merger is a major change, and change is stressful. The technical details of a merger must be well thought out, and the first meeting of the new organization's board and the first day the two original groups' staffs work together must be made as comfortable as possible.

Mission Matters When Merging: A Case Study

During a period of transition, an organization was approached about a merger. Rather than consider merging as a solution to their problems, the board and an interim executive elected to focus on correcting the agency's administrative shortcomings. Then, from a new position of strength, they systematically pursued the option of merger with an organization with similar mission and goals. To understand why a merger made sense for this nonprofit, it is important to appreciate the organization's needs, unique circumstances, traditions, and history.

Description. Pathways for Women was organized in Snohomish County, Washington, in 1976 under the name World for Women. It offered counseling and educational programs for homemakers reentering the workforce. Over the years, the needs of women changed; a growing number of homeless women with children were not effectively accommodated by the existing social services system. Pathways responded by adding a housing program that included rental assistance and transitional and emergency housing.

In 1993, Pathways opened its own eighteen-unit residential housing facility. The new shelter provides housing for women in transition and also contains the organization's administrative and program offices. Pathways' comprehensive program includes classes and workshops on parenting and life skills; counseling, support, and recovery groups; employment assistance in the form of job counseling, job placement, and job search strategies; and outreach activities.

The organization's annual budget is approximately $600,000; 28 percent of this comes from the United Way, 50 percent from government contracts, and the remainder from private funding sources. Pathways employs fourteen full-time equivalent staff.

Background. The organization ran into difficulties in January 1995 after a number of administrative shortcomings had accumulated. The organization's problems centered around a lack of strong leadership from either the board or the executive; unclear roles and expectations for these leaders; ineffective communications between them; and a lack of operational systems for the organization (there was no strategic plan, salary administration plan, or evaluation system for the staff, executive, or board). In particular, the board-executive relationship had become dysfunctional. When a vote of confidence for the executive was taken, staff and board members were split. The divisiveness became intolerable, and the executive left the agency.

At this time, the board was approached by a mental health agency about a merger between the two nonprofits. This was a new idea for the board. As the board chair said, "This turned out to be an opportunity; it was fortunate because it led us to consider an alternative plan of action. We were faced with hiring a new executive or an interim one, or now possibly taking a life rope and merging with another agency that had a strong executive in place who offered administrative credentials that we thought Pathways needed." In evaluating the agency that proposed the merger, the board came to the conclusion that it was not a natural fit: "Their mission didn't really match ours. While we both served some of the same population, their focus on who they were trying to help was quite different. They were a much larger organization, but by absorbing Pathways they sought our organization's identity in the community. We felt our mission would be diminished or lost in the process, so we walked away from that one."

The board hired an interim executive with the expertise to assess the entire organization's operations, implement necessary changes, work with the board to help clarify roles, and explore other merger opportunities. In about four months, superfluous staff were eliminated and administrative systems were established. The board trimmed down from fourteen to seven, committed members, who remained open and receptive to a merger but did not feel pressured to search. Their evaluation of prospective partners focused on agencies in the same county that provided assistance to women in crisis or who were homeless.

Reasons for considering a merger.   The primary benefit to Pathways of a merger was administrative savings; the salaries and benefits of at least one chief executive and fund-raiser could be eliminated, as well as one agency's insurance, bookkeeping, and auditing costs.

Additionally, Pathways had problems attracting quality board members, or those with corporate expertise. The board chair felt Pathway's location was one factor, because the county base from which it drew prospective members was small. Another factor was the nature of the organization itself; businesspeople are not as attracted to a small social services board as they are to one that is larger or more prestigious.

From the interim executive's perspective, a merger made sense due to a shrinking resource environment and Pathways' inability to pay competitive executive salaries. "Most nonprofit organizations with a budget around $500,000 are struggling; their equipment is outdated or broken, there's not enough computers, and so forth."

The process. Pathways' most important criterion in considering the prospect of a merger was mission. In reviewing other organizations' missions, Pathways also learned that the "how" was as important to a mission statement as the "what" or the "who." For example, they considered a merger with the Center for Battered Women (CBW) because it served the same clientele and was organized for a similar purpose. However, CBW's mission expressed a more political philosophy; its strong advocacy for women's rights did not coordinate well with Pathways' more "middle of the road" approach.

Another major criterion was identity. The staff and board felt very strongly about retaining Pathways' name. It had taken a long time for the group to establish its credibility and identity in the community, and it did not make sense for the organization to recreate its reputation.

Early in the process, the interim executive met with the United Way of Snohomish County to discuss the agency's interest in a possible merger. The United Way suggested talking to the YWCA, but Pathways dismissed this as an option because the Y was located in another county and Pathways was still talking to CBW. Months later, when the board thought it had run out of options, the interim executive recalled this earlier conversation about the Y. The board suggested the two executives meet; they did and discovered their two missions fit. Nearly a year after the idea of a merger was first introduced, Pathways has reached the final stages of negotiating a merger with the YWCA of King County.

Pathways' mission is to provide support to women and their families during times of transition or crisis in order to promote stability and self-reliance. The YWCA's mission is to advance the quality of life for women of all ages, races, and faiths and their families; in support of this mission, the YWCA provides services to meet critical needs, promote self-sufficiency, and achieve equal opportunity for all people.

The results. The merger is a win-win situation for both organizations. Pathways will retain its name and identity; it will become an outreach program of the YWCA called YWCA/Pathways for Women. Pathways gains access to a broader base of expertise through the Y's staff and board of directors; economies of scale such as reduced administrative overhead, elimination of an executive's salary, and reduced marketing and public relations costs; and opportunities for staff training and promotion and a higher salary structure.

The YWCA's existing corporate structure easily accommodates the addition of a satellite program; it already has outreach programs in two other areas of King County. The Y wanted a program in Snohomish County but was reluctant to invest years of energy and resources to achieve that end. The YWCA gains: expansion into a new county without start-up program costs, an established, credible operation with stable funding (Pathways will raise its own budget); and access to Pathways' community network and resources in Snohomish County.

The board of Pathways will become an advisory board of the YWCA with a program-oriented function. The staff was gratified to learn that the organizational culture of the YWCA was similar to Pathways' and they could continue to work in a relaxed, comfortable environment. Today, the board and staff of Pathways share a sense of excitement about their future.[11]

Pathways is a case in which the merger process infused an organization with new energy, relief from administrative problems, and hope for its future. While this is not the case for all nonprofits, the advantages of the merger for both Pathways and the YWCA were clear; both organizations stood to gain financially, strategically, and programmatically.

IMPROVING NONPROFITS' IMAGE

By necessity, nonprofit organizations today practice many of the following strategic approaches to management, which in some cases run contrary to how the public expects charitable organizations to operate. Some of these have been discussed in this text:

- collaborative approaches to programming
- partnerships and mergers
- joint ventures in fund-raising
- new forms of compensating staff (e.g., benefits packages)
- the formation of subsidiaries

- the formation of income-generating enterprises
- contract arrangements with the government
- the formation of foundations as conduits for charitable contributions.

Public skepticism is a result of ignorance of contemporary nonprofit management practices.[12] The credibility of the nonprofit sector is also marred by scandals within charities, which not only prompt increased government oversight but serve to diminish public trust.

The negative press received by a few nonprofits has a spillover effect on other charitable organizations, just as fraud, waste, and abuse reported in one government agency serves to undermine the credibility of all government agencies. For example, scandal within the United Way of America made headlines nationwide. In February 1992, allegations about the management practices at the United Way of America under the leadership of William Aramony were reported in the *Washington Post*. In particular, Aramony's high salary and lifestyle, and establishment of subsidiary organizations, were questioned; he was accused of using United Way's resources for personal gain. Newspapers across the nation picked up the story, and Aramony resigned amid public outrage and a loss of confidence among his staff. Aramony was not indicted; while his activities were not illegal, they were perceived to be stretching the limits of ethical management practices.

In another widely publicized scandal, the chief executive of the Foundation for New Era Philanthropy was charged with fraud after his giant Ponzi-style scheme unraveled.[13] The Foundation for New Era Philanthropy (Radnor, Pennsylvania) was founded in 1989 as a type of pooled income fund. It promised contributors a 100 percent return on their "gifts" to the Foundation within six months; it offered a matching fund-raising opportunity for nonprofit organizations. The Foundation's executive claimed to have anonymous donors that would match the funds of new contributors. Like Charles Ponzi of Boston seventy-six years before, New Era paid back new contributors with the money received from earlier gifts. In April 1995, it was discovered that New Era was not registered as a foundation, no anonymous donors existed, and contributors' funds were being used as collateral on a $52 million Foundation loan. The Securities and Exchange Commission charged the executive with diverting $4.2 million of the Foundation's funds into businesses he personally owned. Before New Era's scheme fell apart, many prominent individuals and nonprofit organizations had been caught up in its false promises. In its bankruptcy filing, New Era claimed $551 million in liabilities versus $80 million in assets.

There was a time when the charitable status of an organization was sufficient to gain public sympathy, but that perception has changed. At the 1995 annual meeting of the Independent Sector, Lester Salamon, director of the Institute of Policy Studies at Johns Hopkins University, said, "Nonprofit groups should be alarmed by a fraying of public faith in charities and what they do. The nonprofit sector seems to have lost part of its claim on the sympathies of the American public. Like government, it is increasingly viewed not as part of the solution, but as part of the problem." [14]

Bruce Hopkins, a specialist in nonprofit law, laments that there appears to be nostalgia for earlier times when nonprofit organizations were less sophisticated, operated in the red, and were run by a handful of volunteers or a small staff receiving minimum wages.[15] Those who express this sentiment ignore the fact that neither the nonprofit organization nor its clients benefited from operating in such a limited capacity.

The challenge for nonprofit organizations is to systematically demonstrate accountability and educate their stakeholder and the general public about new nonprofit management practices. A nonprofit board must fulfill its oversight role in all areas of accountability, ensure that the organization's appeals for support are justified on the basis of community and human service needs, work to enhance the organization's image in the community, and ensure that its mission and operations are understood.

SUGGESTIONS FOR FURTHER READING

Gillock, R.E., H.L. Smith and N.F. Piland. "For-Profit and Not-for-Profit Mergers: Concerns and Outcomes." *Hospital and Health Services Administration* vol. 31, no. 6: 74–84, 1986.

LaPiana, David. *Nonprofit Mergers.* Washington, D.C.: National Center for Nonprofit Boards, 1994.

Lewis, Fritz C. and Charles R. Chandler. "The Urge to Merge: Common-Sense Approach to Association Consolidation." *Association Management* (March 1993).

Mason, David. *Leading and Managing the Expressive Dimension.* San Francisco: Jossey-Bass Publishers, 1995.

O'Connell, Brian. *Board Overboard: Laughs and Lessons for All But the Perfect Nonprofit.* San Francisco: Jossey-Bass Publishers, 1995.

Salamon, Lester M. *Partners in Public Service: Government-Nonprofit Relations in the Modern Welfare State.* Baltimore: Johns Hopkins University Press, 1995.

Singer, M.I., and J.A. Yankey. "Organizational Metamorphosis: A Study of Eighteen Nonprofit Mergers, Acquisitions, and Consolidations." *Nonprofit Management and Leadership* vol. 1, no. 4 (1991): 357–369.

Appendixes

Appendix A   Types of Tax-Exempt Organizations Under U.S. Law

Appendix B   Immunity from Civil Liability: Section 5, Florida Statute 617.0285 (1987)

Appendix C   Code of Organizational Ethics: The Hospice of the Florida Suncoast

Appendix D   Letter of Agreement: Agency Access Development Project (AADP)

Appendix E   The 9-Box Tool for Assessing Perceptions

Appendix F   Decision Flow: Municipal League

Appendix G   Organizational Cycle: Municipal League/Foundation

Appendix H   Idea-Generating Techniques

Appendix I   Position Specification: Northwest Network for Youth

Appendix A

TYPES OF TAX-EXEMPT ORGANIZATIONS UNDER U.S. LAW

Code Section	Description
501(c)(1)	corporations organized under an act of Congress
501(c)(2)	title-holding companies
501(c)(3)	religious, charitable, educational organizations
501(c)(4)	social welfare, civic leagues
501(c)(5)	labor, agricultural organizations
501(c)(6)	business leagues
501(c)(7)	social and recreational clubs
501(c)(8)	fraternal beneficiary societies
501(c)(9)	voluntary employees' beneficiary societies
501(c)(10)	domestic fraternal beneficiary societies
501(c)(11)	teachers' retirement funds
501(c)(12)	benevolent life insurance associations
501(c)(13)	cemetery companies
501(c)(14)	credit unions
501(c)(15)	mutual insurance companies
501(c)(16)	corporations to finance crop operation
501(c)(17)	supplemental unemployment benefit trusts
501(c)(18)	employee-funded pension trusts
501(c)(19)	war veterans' organizations
501(c)(20)	legal services organizations
501(c)(21)	black lung trusts
501(d)	religious and apostolic organizations
501(e)	cooperative hospital service organizations
501(f)	cooperative service organizations of operating educational organizations
521	farmers' cooperatives

Source: Internal Revenue Service, *Annual Report 1989.*

Appendix B

Officers and Directors of certain corporations and associations not for profit; immunity from civil liability.

1. An officer or director of a non profit organization recognized under Section 501(c)(3) or Section 501(c)(4) or Section 501(c)(6), or of an agricultural or a horticultural organization recognized under Section 501(c)(5), of the Internal Revenue Code of 1986, as amended, is not personally liable for monetary damages to any person for any statement, vote, decision, or failure to take an action, regarding organizational management or policy by an officer or director, unless:

    a. The officer or director breached or failed to perform his duties as an officer or director; and

    b. The officer's or director's breach of, or failure to perform, his duties constitutes:

        1. A violation of the criminal law, unless the officer or director had reasonable cause to believe his conduct was lawful or had no reasonable cause to believe that his conduct was unlawful;

        2. A transaction from which the officer or director derived an improper personal benefit, either directly, or indirectly; or

        3. Recklessness or act of omission which was committed in bad faith or with malicious purpose or in a manner exhibiting wanton and willful disregard of human rights, safety or property.

2. For the purpose of this Section, the term:

    a. "Recklessness" means the acting, or omission to act, in conscious disregard of a risk:

        1. Known, or so obvious that it should have been known, to the officer or director; and

2. Known to the officer or director, or so obvious that it should have been known, to be so great as to make it highly probable that harm would follow from such action or omission.

b. "Director" means a person who serves as director, trustee, or member of the governing board of an organization.

c. "Officer" means a person who serves as an officer without compensation except reimbursement for actual expenses incurred or to be incurred.

Appendix C

CODE OF ORGANIZATIONAL ETHICS: THE HOSPICE OF THE
FLORIDA SUNCOAST

**CODE OF CONDUCT/CONFLICT OF INTEREST/POLICY REGARD-
ING GIFTS TO EMPLOYEES AND VOLUNTEERS.** Every person affiliated with Hospice (including staff and volunteers) is privileged to
serve our patients, families and general publics without the need for personal gain or favors. Employees and volunteers have the responsibility
of serving everyone equally and are not to use the relationships gained
through or because of that service for their personal or professional benefit.

Regarding Conduct—employees and volunteers are at all times to conduct
themselves to our various Hospice publics in a professional manner. As
such, information gained through that relationship shall be deemed private
and confidential and shall be kept within the confines of Hospice. This information includes but is not limited to patient/family information; donor
information; information gained through research; agency documents including strategic plans, marketing plans, etc.; financial information related
to the agency, etc. It is further understood that such confidential information is owned or entrusted to The Hospice of the Florida Suncoast.

Regarding Conflict of Interest—employees and volunteers are not to cap-
italize on their Hospice relationships in order to further their personal or
professional goals or gains. In addition, employees and volunteers are directed to avoid potential conflict of interest situations and/or appearance
of conflict situations. These situations include but are not limited to promoting personal business opportunities and/or vendor products to Hospice; serving in various capacities for our Hospice publics (including volunteers) as Personal Representatives in wills and estates; agreeing to be
named as a Healthcare surrogates, etc.

Regarding Gifts—employees and volunteers are prohibited from accepting money, items of personal property, gifts, donations, loans or anything

else of value from any of our Hospice publics. This policy includes gifts and bequests made by our patients/families through their estate or through any other post-mortem device. Should circumstances arise wherein our patients and/or families affirmatively inform a volunteer or employee that they wish to show appreciation for care provided, employees and volunteers may inform the patients and/or families that Hospice accepts charitable contributions.

The Hospice of the Florida Suncoast also recognizes that uncomfortable situations may however occur wherein family members would genuinely be hurt by refusal of a gift. As such, should situations arise whereby family members have *already* purchased an in-kind gift with an estimated value under $20.00 (candy, flowers, etc.) it may be accepted on behalf of the entire team with supervisor's approval. Such supervisor shall also keep a log of accepted gifts and report same to the Development & Community Relations Department for proper gift acknowledgment and recognition. Under no circumstances, however, shall employees and volunteers accept monetary gifts.

Any situations arising not covered by the above policy shall be discussed with the Development & Community Relations Director/and or the Executive Director or the Chairman of the Board at Hospice.

Signed _____

Date _____

Printed Name _____

Policy 3/95

Source: The Hospice of the Florida Suncoast. Reprinted with permission.

Appendix D

LETTER OF AGREEMENT: AGENCY ACCESS DEVELOPMENT
PROJECT (AADP)

Dated:_____

BETWEEN

Agency: _____

and the

UNITED WAY OF THE LOWER MAINLAND

The agency names_____as its "Change Agent" to participate in the Agency Access Development Project.

PREAMBLE

PURPOSE

The purpose of this agreement is to outline the respective commitments of
the agency and the United Way of the Lower Mainland as the agency com-
mits itself to a process of multicultural organizational change.

PRINCIPLES

The principles underlying the Agency Access Development Project are:

▶ Self-help - that agencies are in the best position to know what
they need and that agencies can learn from one another and support each other in a change process;

▶ Integration - multiculturalism needs to be integrated and incorporated within the organizations' ongoing planning
and operations; not as a separate project;

▶ Sustainability - multicultural organizational change should be sustained over the long term, and not just the duration
of this project.

CONDITIONS

Based upon research and experience the conditions required for multicultural organizational change to be successful are:

▶   There is commitment from the top.

▶   There is clarity on what needs to be changed.

▶   The process is internally managed.

▶   The process is participatory.

▶   The process is supported by training.

▶   The process is knowledge-based.

▶   The change is reflected in policies and procedures.

▶   Goals are action-oriented and measurable.

▶   Resources are targeted.

▶   The action plan has built-in accountability.

OUTCOMES

For the purposes of this project, the indicators of successful multicultural organizational change are:

1. The agency has developed a multicultural and anti-racist policy which embraces all agency operations.

    ▶   The agency has developed a multicultural and anti-racism policy;

    ▶   The policy has been passed by the Board;

    ▶   The policy addresses issues of reflectiveness of staff and volunteers, appropriateness of program services and communications to diverse ethno-racial groups, and handling of racist incidents;

    ▶   There has been public affirmation of the policy.

    ▶   This policy is included within the agency's overall policies;

2. The agency has developed an action plan incorporating multicultural and anti-racism objectives throughout its operations.

    ▶   The action plan has been prepared and is being followed;

    ▶   The action plan impacts all the agency's operations;

    ▶   There is a procedure for monitoring and evaluating the results of the action plan;

▶ The action plan is incorporated/integrated into the larger action plan of the organization.

3. The agency's programs, services and communications are accessible to the community it is mandated to serve;

▶ The agency has determined the barriers and gaps in programs, services and communications with respect to accessibility to the community that it is mandated to serve;

▶ The agency has taken steps to address identified barriers and gaps in programs, services and communications with respect to accessibility to the community that it is mandated to serve;

4. The agency has achieved appropriate representation of diverse ethno-racial groups within its volunteer and staff structure. (The definition of "appropriate" to be based on general community demographics, population served, and/or strategic objectives of the agency).

▶ The agency has conducted a survey to determine the racial and ethnic composition of its Board, senior management, staff, volunteers and clients. The staff survey has also examined its recruitment, hiring and promotion practices;

▶ The agency has compared the demographic profile of its Board, senior management, staff, volunteers and clients to that of its catchment area and target group;

▶ The agency has a recruitment and hiring strategy which incorporates in its goals ethno-racial reflectiveness of Board, staff and volunteers.

AGREEMENT

A. UNITED WAY COMMITMENT

United Way of the Lower Mainland agrees to assist the above named agency, in the process of multicultural organizational change from the date of this contract until December 1994 (approximately two years) by providing:

1. <u>Information Sharing/Networking</u>

    ▶ Opportunities for networking through clusters.

    ▶ Staff support to clusters re: meeting place, scheduling, etc.

    ▶ Information/community demographics relevant to conducting a barrier analysis.

    ▶ Resource information on multicultural organizational change as shared by other "clusters," i.e. cross-cluster sharing.

    ▶ Resource information on multicultural organizational change experienced by agencies in other cities, i.e. Halifax, Toronto, Calgary.

    ▶ Identification of common critical issues/problems experienced by agencies in the non-profit sector generally, and problem solving around those issues.

    ▶ Opportunities for practical, hands on problem-solving in a neutral setting.

    ▶ Provision of resource persons, samples, etc., as they are identified by clusters.

    ▶ Provision of "Equity, Access, Diversity" guides at a reduced cost.

2. <u>Training and Skill Acquisition—Formal and Informal</u>

    ▶ Agency "Change Agents" will be trained on the multicultural organizational change process, through acquiring skills, tools, resources. In addition opportunity will be provided for practical problem solving as it pertains to the Change Agents' own experience.

    ▶ Formal training workshops, ranging from half day sessions to two day sessions, will be provided to all Change Agents.

    ▶ Formal training workshops will cover a range of topics and formats, depending upon the training focus. The series will generally cover the following topics:

        ▶ Orientation to principles of Multicultural Organizational Change
        ▶ Internal Assessment/Barrier Analysis
        ▶ Community Consultation
        ▶ Developing Change Strategies
        ▶ Achieving Staff Reflectiveness
        ▶ Recruiting and Maintaining Volunteers
        ▶ Handling of Racist Incidents and Policy Development

B. AGENCY COMMITMENT

1. The agency agrees to participate in the Agency Access Development Project from the date of this Contract until December 1994 (about 2 years). In doing so, the agency acknowledges that it is committing itself to a process of multicultural organizational change.

2. <u>Change Agent</u> : The agency agrees that the Change Agent named in this document:

   2.1 is the Executive Director or a Senior Staff person of the agency;

   2.2 is the key person responsible for facilitating the multicultural organizational change process within the agency;

   2.3 has direct access to the Board of Directors;

   2.4 has a personal commitment to the multicultural organizational change process

   2.5 will participate regularly in the cluster meetings to share information/knowledge and to learn from others;

   2.6 will attend designated training sessions.

   2.7 has the agency support to facilitate the multicultural organizational change process within the agency.

3. <u>Multicultural Organizational Change Committee</u>

   3.1 The agency agrees to strike a Multicultural Organizational Change Committee (if it does not already have one);

   3.2 This Committee should include the "Change Agent," at least one Board member and whoever else the agency deems appropriate;

   3.3 The Committee should provide leadership and policy direction on multicultural organizational change within the agency, and report regularly to the Board of Directors.

4. <u>Training Participation</u>

   4.1 The agency agrees that key staff & Board members will participate in designated training sessions provided through the Agency Access Development Project program. The Change Agent will attend all training sessions.

5. <u>Formal Evaluation</u>

    5.1   The agency recognizes that the Agency Access Development Project is a pilot project and that the findings may be useful to other agencies. Therefore, the agency agrees to participate in a formal evaluation process over the duration of the project. The evaluation instruments are those developed by United Way's agents, Steven Goldberg and Associates, and are designed to measure the progress and effectiveness of this model of multi-cultural organizational change.

Agency: _____   Date:_____

Signed: _____   _____
                    President   **Executive Director**

United Way of the Lower Mainland

Signed: Date:_____

_____   _____
                    President   **Executive Director**

Source: United Way of Lower Mainland, Burnaby B.C. Canada. Reprinted with permission.

Appendix E

THE 9-BOX TOOL FOR ASSESSING PERCEPTIONS

A tool to assess a group's perception of the probability that a trend will continue, and what its potential impact on an organization might be.

Trend or Issue: _____

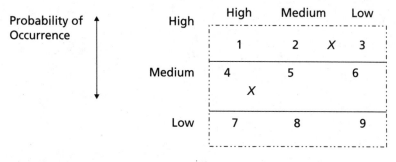

Instructions:

1. Draw 9-box diagram on a flip chart.
2. Ask each group member to mark an X on the chart in the box where he or she thinks the trend (or issue) in question may fall. (Or, do this individually and tabulate the responses on the flip chart.) For example, if the trend is a more ethnically diverse population, and a member feels that there is a high probability this trend will continue but it will have only a moderate impact on the organization, he would draw an X in box 2. If another feels the trend has a medium probability for continuing and a potentially high impact on the organization, she would put an X in box 4, and so on.
3. After everyone has marked their choices, the group can quickly gauge if there is a consensus about whether a trend/issue warrants attention. A majority of Xs in boxes 1, 2, and 4 might signal a potential opportunity (or threat) that requires in-depth discussion and planning. Or, the

group may decide that if the Xs are not clustered in cell 1, the trend/issue does not deserve special attention. Each group should establish its own criteria for significance and determine which cell clusters merit attention.

4. Repeat this exercise for each major trend/issue identified in scanning the organization's environment.

Remember, these are only perceptions!

Appendix F

Mission:

The mission of The Municipal League of King County is to (1) promote good government that is open, effective, and accountable in order to improve the caliber of public officials and the quality of public decisions and (2) to assist our community to identify and efficiently solve its problems and reach its goal through active and broad-based participation of citizens in government.

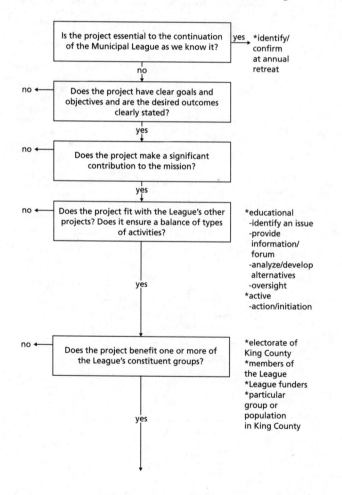

169

A "no" on most of these points suggests the need to further refine the proposed project. In the first analysis, the relative balance of "yes" and "no" answers must be weighed in order to reach a decision.

The appropriate committee first uses this decision process, bringing forward recommended project to the Executive Committee. The process is again applied by the Executive Committee, and a recommendation made to the Board. The Board must finally adopt a project.

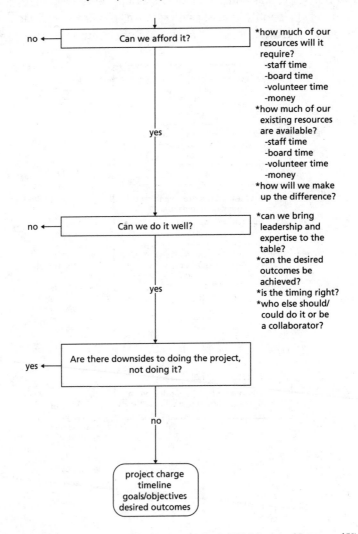

Appendix G

ORGANIZATIONAL CYCLE: MUNICIPAL LEAGUE/FOUNDATION

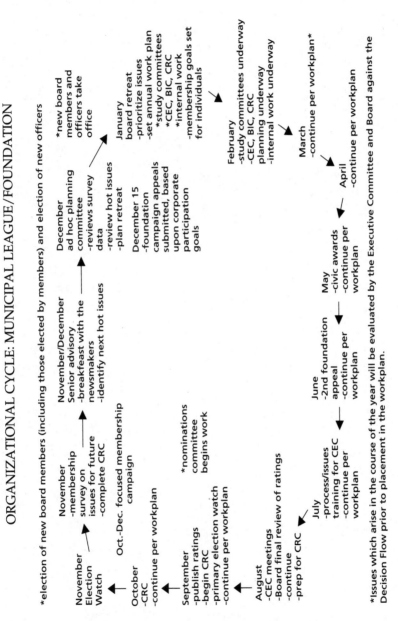

*election of new board members (including those elected by members) and election of new officers

November Election Watch

November
-membership survey on issues for future
-complete CRC

November/December
Senior advisory
-breakfeast with the newsmakers
-identify next hot issues

December
ad hoc planning committee
-reviews survey data
-review hot issues
-plan retreat

*new board members and officers take office

January
board retreat
-prioritize issues
-set annual work plan
*study committees
*CEC, BIC, CRC
*internal work
-membership goals set for individuals

Oct.-Dec. focused membership campaign

October
-CRC
-continue per workplan

December 15
-foundation campaign appeals submitted, based upon corporate participation goals

February
-study committees underway
-CEC, BIC, CRC planning underway
-internal work underway

September
-publish ratings
-begin CRC
-primary election watch
-continue per workplan

*nominations committee begins work

March
-continue per workplan*

August
-CEC meetings
-Board final review of ratings
-continue
-prep for CRC

July
-process/issues training for CEC
-continue per workplan

June
-2nd foundation appeal
-continue per workplan

May
-civic awards
-continue per workplan

April
-continue per workplan

*Issues which arise in the course of the year will be evaluated by the Executive Committee and Board against the Decision Flow prior to placement in the workplan.

Source: Municipal League of King County. Copyright © 1993 Municipal League of King County.

Appendix H

IDEA-GENERATING TECHNIQUES

Strategic planning and collaborative decision-making require the generation of many ideas. The following outline offers some techniques.

1. Piggybacking: Build one idea onto another as they are given, base several ideas on one prior idea.

For example, if one person suggests adding a bookmobile to the library's service, the next person might suggest that it make scheduled stops at nursing homes and hospitals; a third person may add that the bookmobile should be painted in bright colors to attract attention, a fourth might suggest that elementary school children be invited to create a design, and so forth.

2. Visual Displays: Show every idea.

For example, participants' ideas are written on large sheets of paper and displayed around the room. The visual display allows everyone to see what has already been suggested, prompts related ideas, and demonstrates that everyone's thoughts are important.

3. Force Fitting: Join two or more new ideas to create an alternative one.

4. Magnifying or Minimizing: Enlarge or shrink existing ideas in order to create a new idea or make an idea workable.

For example, someone suggests opening an extension program in another part of the community. Rather than dismiss the idea as too costly, the suggestion could be "minimized" by considering as an alternative an outreach program offered two days a week, offerings of programs in cooperation with other agencies, and so forth.

5. Humor and Play: Encourage crazy and silly ideas to stimulate creativity.

6. Reaching a Specified Number: Continue creating ideas until a certain target number is reached.

For example, the group keeps going until it has 20 ideas posted.

7. Setting a Time Limit: Stop generating ideas at some specified time. For example, allow only 15, 20 or 30 minutes for discussion.

Appendix I

POSITION SPECIFICATION

Position Title	Executive Director
Reports To	Eleven Member Board of Directors
Salary Range	Negotiable, between $31,500 and $42,000 per year, depending upon qualifications and experience.
Benefits	The Network Executive Director receives a benefit package that includes: vacation, sick leave, paid holidays, SEP Individual Retirement Account, health insurance, and life insurance.
Budget	The annual budget for fiscal year 1995 is close to $200,000. Approximately 75% of this amount is from the Administration for Children, Youth and Families, 10% is from donations, 8% from membership dues, and 7% is from training and conference fees.
The Organization	*Mission*

The Northwest Network for Youth affirms the value of all youth by creating an on-going forum for professional development and support through training and technical assistance to organizations and individuals serving at-risk youth.

The Northwest Network encompasses the states of Alaska, Idaho, Oregon, and Washington: Federal Region X.

The Network accomplishes its mission through four principle programs: providing technical assistance to youth serving agencies by networking, and managing

175

the Regional Resource Library; holding training seminars and an annual conference, *Pacific Northwest Youth Summit;* publishing newsletters and other documents; and advocating for systems change on a state and national level.

History

The Network was conceived in the mid 1980's by a group of runaway shelter directors, in the four state region, who were concerned about high-risk youth. The group concluded that early intervention, training in life skills, and repair of emotional damage could best be provided by a network of agencies exchanging information and expertise. The Network was incorporated as a 501(c)(3) nonprofit agency in 1986. The Network was located in Ashland, Oregon, until 1993, when it was moved to Seattle, Washington.

Also in 1993 was the first Annual Scholarship Auction. The proceeds from this annual auction provides funding to promote participation of youth at regional and national conferences.

In the past nine years, the Network has grown to 39 member agencies. The Network will celebrate its 10th anniversary in 1996.

Related Agencies   The Network maintains alliances and collaborative relationships with the following youth serving agencies:

- National Network for Youth
- Regional Network Training and Technical Assistance Providers
- Administration for Children, Youth and Families
- National 4-H Council
- Girls Incorporated
- National Resource Center for Youth Services
- Center for Youth Development and Policy Research
- Institute of Cultural Affairs
- Children First for Oregon

- The Children's Alliance
- National Clearinghouse on Runaway and Homeless Youth
- National Runaway Switchboard

The Position

The Executive Director of the Network is employed in an exempt position; the Executive Director is appointed by and serves at the pleasure of the Board of Directors, and reports to the Board Chair. The Director supervises a staff of three. He/She works directly with the staff, the Executive Committee as an ex-officio member, and its several standing committees to establish policies, initiate new programs, and maintain existing ones.

The Executive Director is responsible for program administration, the development of administration of standards and procedures related to personnel and staff development, the Network's budget, and its facilities. The Director is expected to assume a leadership role in maintaining cooperative relationships with youth serving agencies nationally and regionally, and act as spokesperson for the Network with all stakeholders.

The responsibilities of the Executive Director include, but are not limited to, the following:

Organizational Management and Leadership
1. Advise the Board and carry out tasks assigned by the Board.
2. Personnel management, i.e., oversee the recruitment, hiring, training, supervision, evaluation, and termination of staff.
3. Serve as liaison between staff and Board members.
4. Coordinate with the Board's Committee Chairs and staff to oversee activities, including:
   a. grant applications,
   b. management of grants,
   c. program and training evaluations,

      d.   community relations,
      e.   Regional Resource Library,
      f.   cluster training,
      g.   annual conference,
      h.   special projects, and
      i.   fiscal management.

5. Serve as spokesperson and make public presentations on behalf of the Network.
6. Manage and develop annual budget for Board approval, and revisions as necessary.
7. Manage Network finances and reporting.
8. Facilitate annual Board retreat to include strategic planning process in order to accomplish short and long term goals and objectives.
9. Coordinate all meetings of the Board.
10. Provide quarterly report to Board Members.
11. Oversee the preparation of the Annual Report of Network activities and fiscal reports.
12. Coordinate work on annual audit.

Fund Development

1. Supervise fundraising activities, following Board approval policy.
2. Oversee the preparation and submission of funding proposals to aid in the accomplishment of Network goals and objectives.
3. Oversee reporting to funding sources as required.
4. Determine funding priorities of the Board.

Priorities & Issues The new Executive Director will:

Board Relations

- Work with the Board to implement a long-term vision and organizational plan.
- Work with the Board to ensure greater participation by member organizations.
- Work with the Board to enhance the diversity of the Network on an on-going basis.

Program Development

- Work with the Board and staff to stay abreast of emerging issues that impact youth and family services.
- Continue to enhance the Network's image as a regional leader in training and youth services.
- Promote a greater exchange of information between and with youth serving agencies, locally, regionally and nationally.
- Collaborate with other groups on common issues and topics.
- Promote Community Youth Development.

Operations

- Continue the sense of team within Network staff.
- Review job descriptions to determine if they are relevant as the Network continues to change.
- Develop a working knowledge of the Network's records, resources, funding sources, and grant recipients.
- Strengthen the Network's information links with the other nine Regional Networks, including a Peer Review.

Building Community Awareness

- Position the Network to be the leading trainer for youth workers in Region X.
- Quickly become a visible and persuasive facilitator of youth and family issues.
- Develop connections with all Network stakeholders in each of the four states and nationally.
- Continue to reach a broad public, including legislators and public officials, through *On Line* and other publications.

Source: Courtesy of Waldron & Company and Northwest Network for Youth. Used with permission.

Notes

PROLOGUE

1. Paula Rae Brody, interview by author, 19 October 1995. Paula Rae Brody has just finished writing a book on the history and projects of CCAM at the request of the former Official Hostess Mama C. Tamanda Kadzamira. Mrs. Brody is the wife of the Consul General Emeritus for Malawi in the United States. She and her husband lived in Malawi for more than ten years.

CHAPTER ONE: MODELS OF GOVERNANCE AND LEADERSHIP

1. Cyril O. Houle, *Governing Boards: Their Nature and Nurture* (San Francisco: Jossey-Bass Publishers, 1989).
2. Houle, *Governing Boards,* 8.
3. John Carver, *Boards That Make a Difference* (San Francisco: Jossey-Bass Publishers, 1990), 28.
4. Carver, *Boards That Make a Difference,* xiii.
5. Carver, *Boards That Make a Difference,* 34–35.
6. Miriam M. Wood, "Is Governing Board Behavior Cyclical?" *Nonprofit Management and Leadership* 3, 2 (winter 1992): 139–163.
7. Wood, "Is Governing Board Behavior Cyclical?" 158.
8. Richard P. Chait, *How to Help Your Board Govern More and Manage Less* (Washington, D.C.: National Center for Nonprofit Boards, 1993).
9. Richard P. Chait and Barbara E. Taylor, "Charting the Territory of Nonprofit Boards," *Harvard Business Review* 89, 1 (January–February 1989): 44–54.

CHAPTER TWO: ACCOUNTABILITY: A BOARD'S FIDUCIARY OBLIGATIONS

1. David H. Rosenbloom, *Public Administration: Understanding Management, Politics, and Law in the Public Sector,* 3rd ed. (New York: McGraw Hill, 1993).
2. Carver, *Boards That Make a Difference.*
3. Carver, *Boards That Make a Difference.*

4. Seattle-King County Bar Association, "How To Form a Nonprofit Corporation in Washington State" (1992): 19–21.

5. Seattle-King County Bar Association, "How To Form a Nonprofit Corporation in Washington State": 10.

6. Seattle-King County Bar Association, "How To Form a Nonprofit Corporation in Washington State": 40.

7. Bruce R. Hopkins, *A Legal Guide to Starting and Managing A Nonprofit Organization*, 2nd ed. (New York: John Wiley & Sons, 1993), 244–248.

8. Bruce Hopkins, "Law and Taxation," in *The Nonprofit Management Handbook: Operating Policies and Practices,* Tracy D. Connors, ed. (New York: John Wiley & Sons, 1993), 874.

9. An annual football game between rivals University of Washington and Washington State University.

10. Interview by author, 15 March 1995, Everett, WA.

11. Salvation Army position statement, document no. A-32 (May 1985), 6.

12. Terry L. Cooper, *The Responsible Administrator: An Approach to Ethics for the Administrative Role,* 3rd ed. (San Francisco: Jossey-Bass Publishers, 1990), 13.

13. Interview by author, 15 March 1995, Seattle WA.

14. Carver, *Boards That Make a Difference,* 92.

15. Peter Dobkin Hall, *Inventing the Nonprofit Sector and Other Essays on Philanthropy, Voluntarism, and Nonprofit Organizations* (Baltimore: Johns Hopkins University Press, 1992).

CHAPTER THREE: STRUCTURING A BOARD FOR MAXIMUM EFFECTIVENESS

1. Harleigh B. Trecker, *Citizen Boards at Work* (New York: Association Press, 1970), 143.

2. Larry H. Slesinger and Richard L. Moyers, *A Snapshot of America's Nonprofit Boards: Results of a National Survey* (Washington, D.C.: National Center for Nonprofit Boards, 1995), 4.

3. Slesinger and Moyers, *A Snapshot of America's Nonprofit Boards,* 8.

4. Slesinger and Moyers, *A Snapshot of America's Nonprofit Boards,* 8.

5. William G. Bowen, *Inside the Boardroom* (New York: John Wiley & Sons, 1994), 40.

6. Brian O'Connell, *Effective Leadership in Voluntary Organizations* (New York: Walker & Company, 1981), 81.

7. Bowen, *Inside the Boardroom.*

8. Rikki Abzug, Paul J. DiMaggio, Bradford H. Gray, Chul Hee Kang, and Michael Useem, *Changes in the Structure and Composition of Nonprofit Boards of Trustees: Cases from Boston and Cleveland, 1925–1985* (PONPO Working Paper No. 173, Institute for Social and Policy Studies, Yale University, April 1992).

9. Hall, *Inventing the Nonprofit Sector.*

10. United Way of the Lower Mainland, Burnaby, British Columbia, Canada "Agency Access Development Project: Action Plan," report (September 1992).

11. Jennifer M. Rutledge, *Building Board Diversity* (Washington, D.C.: National Center for Nonprofit Boards, 1994), 44.

12. Rutledge, *Building Board Diversity.*

13. United Way of the Lower Mainland, Burnaby, British Columbia, "Agency Access Development Project."

14. National Advisory Council of the University of Utah, Salt Lake City, UT., By-laws, Art. III, sec. 3.

15. Interview by author, 8 May 1995, Seattle WA.

16. Shriners General Office, Tampa, FL., "A Short History of the Ancient Arabic Order Nobles of the Mystic Shrine," report (March 1995): 23.

17. The Hospice of the Florida Suncoast, Largo, FL, "The Hospice of the Florida Suncoast Board Roles and Responsibilities": 1995.

18. Institute director, interview by author, June 1995, Largo FL.

CHAPTER FOUR: ORGANIZING THE BOARD'S WORK

1. Houle, *Governing Boards.*

2. Tracy Daniel Connors, "The Board of Directors," in *The Nonprofit Organization Handbook,* Tracy Daniel Connors, ed. (New York: McGraw-Hill, 1980).

3. Slesinger and Moyers, *A Snapshot of America's Nonprofit Boards,* 15.

4. Carver, *Boards That Make a Difference.*

5. Carver, *Boards That Make a Difference.*

6. Carver, *Boards That Make a Difference.*

7. Carver, *Boards That Make a Difference.*

8. Bowen, *Inside the Boardroom.*

9. Benjamin Sprafkin, "How to Become a More Effective Board Member," in *Institute for Board Members* (Richmond: Virginia Commonwealth University, School of Social Work, March–April 1968), 25.

10. Sprafkin, "How To Become a More Effective Board Member."

CHAPTER FIVE: THE CORE RESPONSIBILITIES OF A NONPROFIT BOARD

1. George Steiner, *Top Management Planning* (New York: Macmillan Publishing, 1969), 176.

2. Steiner, *Top Management Planning;* Chait and Taylor, "Charting the Territory."

3. Carver, *Boards That Make a Difference.*

4. Paul C. Nutt and Robert W. Backoff, *Strategic Management of Public and Third Sector Organizations* (San Francisco: Jossey-Bass Publishers, 1992).

5. Nutt and Backoff, *Strategic Management of Public and Third Sector Organizations.*

6. John M. Bryson, *Strategic Planning for Public and Nonprofit Organizations* (San Francisco: Jossey-Bass Publishers, 1988).

7. Shriners Imperial Council, "Men's Leisure Time," report on a research study commissioned from Louis Harris & Associates (Tampa, Shriners General Offices): 14–15.

8. Shriners Imperial Council, "Men's Leisure Time": 1–2.

9. Robert J. Myers, Peter Ufford, Mary-Scot Magill, and Deborah McPhedran, *On-Site Analysis*, 2nd ed., 1989 (Revised excerpt from: United Way of the Lower Mainland, Burnaby, British Columbia, Canada), 5.

10. Executive Director of the United Way of the Lower Mainland, interview by author, Vancouver, B.C., Canada, 3 November 1995.

11. Bowen, *Inside the Boardroom*, 124–125.

12. Slesinger and Moyers, *A Snapshot of America's Nonprofit Boards*, 5.

13. Third Sector Consulting, interview by author, Seattle, WA, 8 May 1995.

14. Hall, *Inventing the Nonprofit Sector.*

15. Mark I. Wilson, ed. "The State of Nonprofit Michigan 1994" report (East Lansing: Michigan State University, 1995).

16. Putnam Barber, "Nonprofits in Washington" (Seattle: Department of Community, Trade, and Economic Development, 1994).

17. Karen W. Arenson, "If Welfare Is Cut, Will Charities Close Gap?," the *New York Times* (reported in the *Seattle Times*, 4 June 1995), A1.

18. American Fund Raising Counsel, "Giving USA 1994," report.

19. *Chronicle of Philanthropy*, 2 November 1995, 32.

20. Howard Gershen, *A Guide For Giving* (New York: Pantheon Books, 1990).

21. James Joseph, *Remaking America*. (San Francisco: Jossey-Bass Publishers, 1995).

CHAPTER SIX: BUILDING A COOPERATIVE SPIRIT

1. Executive Director of United Way of Lower Mainland, interview by author, Vancouver, B.C., Canada, 3 November 1995.

2. Robert D. Herman and Richard D. Heimovics, "An Investigation of Leadership Skill Differences in Chief Executives of Nonprofit Organizations," *American Review of Public Administration* 20, 2 (June 1990): 107.

3. Herman and Heimovics, "An Investigation of Leadership Skill Differences in Chief Executives of Nonprofit Organizations."

4. Herman and Heimovics, "An Investigation of Leadership Skill Differences in Chief Executives of Nonprofit Organizations," 121.

5. Interview by author, November 1995.

6. Carver, *Boards That Make a Difference*, 125.

7. Houle, *Governing Boards*, 12.

8. Houle, *Governing Boards.*

9. Interview by author, October 1995.

10. Executive Director of Girls Inc. of Greater Santa Barbara, interview by author, 20 October 1995.

CHAPTER SEVEN: EFFECTIVE BOARD MEETINGS

1. John E. Tropman, "Holding Effective Board Meetings," in *Nonprofit Boards: A Practical Guide to Roles, Responsibilities, and Performance,* by Diane J. Duca (Phoenix: Oryx Press, 1986).

2. Carver, *Boards That Make a Difference.*

3. Carver, Boards That Make a Difference, 169–170.

4. Rodney Napier and Mattik Gershenfeld, *Groups, Theory and Experience.* (Boston: Houghton Mifflin, 1993).

5. Alvin Zander, *Making Groups Effective,* 2nd ed. (San Francisco: Jossey-Bass Publishers, 1994).

6. The Municipal League of King County consists of a 501(c)(4) organization and a smaller 501(c)(3) educational foundation.

7. Carver, *Boards That Make a Difference.*

8. Chait, *How to Help Your Board Govern More,* 6.

9. John E. Tropman, *Effective Meetings: Improving Group Decision-Making* (Thousand Oaks: Sage Publications, 1980).

10. John L. Adams, *Conceptual Blockbusting,* 3rd ed. (Reading: Addison-Wesley Publishing, 1986).

11. Adams, *Conceptual Blockbusting.*

12. Bob Myers, Gary McCarthy, and Deborah McPhedran, "Application of the On-Site Analysis Process in Day-to-Day Management," a report (Etobicoke, Ontario: On-Site Analysis Associates, 1992).

13. Wendell French, in *Organizational Behavior,* 5th ed., Don Hellriegel, John W. Slocum, Jr., and Richard W. Woodman, eds. (New York: West Publishing, 1989).

14. Myers et al, "Application of the On-Site Analysis Process in Day-to-Day Management," 33.

CHAPTER EIGHT: MAINTAINING FOCUS ON MISSION

1. E.B. Knauft, Renee A. Berger and Sandra T. Gray, *Profiles of Excellence: Achieving Success in the Nonprofit Sector* (San Francisco: Jossey-Bass Publishers, 1991), 119–120.

2. Phil Nudelman, "This Place is a Zoo," *Seattle Post-Intelligencer,* Sunday, 17 September 1995, E1.

3. Ann Landers, *Seattle Post-Intelligencer,* Sunday, 17 September 1995.

4. Corporate Council for the Arts, Seattle, WA, "Report of the Role Committee," 1989, 1.

5. Peter Donnelly, President (chief executive officer) of CCA, interview by author, 22 March 1995.

6. Javier Diaz-Albertini cited in *The Road from Rio: Sustainable Development and the Nongovernmental Movement in the Third World,* Julie Fisher (Westport: Praeger, 1993), 166.

7. Virginia A. Hodgkinson and Russy D. Sumariwalla, "The Nonprofit Sector and the New Global Community: Issues and Challenges," in *The Nonprofit Sector in the Global Community,* ed. Kathleen D. McCarthy, Virginia A. Hodgkinson, Russy D. Sumariwalla, and associates (San Francisco: Jossey-Bass Publishers, 1992), 485–507.

8. Fisher, *The Road from Rio.*

9. Fisher, *The Road from Rio,* 165.

CHAPTER NINE: NEW CHALLENGES FOR NONPROFIT BOARDS

1. Frederick S. Lane, "Government Relations and the Nonprofit Manager," *Nonprofit Management and Leadership* 4, 1 (fall 1993): 117–121.

2. Virginia Hodgkinson, Richard W. Lyman, and associates, *The Future of the Nonprofit Sector* (San Francisco: Jossey-Bass Publishers, 1989), 10.

3. Lane, "Government Relations and the Nonprofit Manager."

4. Sharon L. Harlan and Judith R. Saidel, "Board Members' Influence on the Government-Nonprofit Relationship," *Nonprofit Management and Leadership* 5, 2 (winter 1994): 174.

5. Harlan and Saidel, "Board Members' Influence on the Government-Nonprofit Relationship": 176.

6. Hall, *Inventing the Nonprofit Sector.*

7. Hall, *Inventing the Nonprofit Sector*, 265.

8. Richard D. Heimovics and Robert D. Herman, "Responsibility for Critical Events in Nonprofit Organizations," *Nonprofit and Voluntary Sector Quarterly* 19, 1 (1990): 59–72.

9. President of Seattle-King County Planned Parenthood, interview by author, 13 April 1995.

10. Hillel Schmid, "Merging Nonprofit Organizations: Analysis of a Case Study," *Nonprofit Management and Leadership* 5, 4 (summer 1995): 377–391.

11. President of the board of directors and Interim Director of Pathways for Women, interviews by author, October 1995.

12. Bruce Hopkins, preface to *The United Way Scandal,* by John S. Glaser (New York: John Wiley & Sons, 1994).

13. Steve Wulf, "Too Good to be True" *Time,* 29 May 1995, 34.

14. Lester Salamon, quoted in "Nonprofit Leaders Urged to Face Financial Image Crisis," Susan Gray, *Chronicle of Philanthropy* 2 November 1995, 61.

15. Hopkins, preface to *The United Way Scandal.*

Index

Accountability. *See also* Ethics; Legal issues
board and executive, 18–20
introduction to, 17–18
Advisory bodies, 43–46
Agendas, setting focused, 105–107
Agua para el Pueblo, 127
Alliances, collaboration and strategic, 140–143
American Zoo and Aquarium Association, 119
Aramony, William, 149
Articles of incorporation, 20
Arts United of Puget Sound, 104
Asian Pacific Women's Caucus, 104

Bell-shaped agenda, 107
Ben & Jerry's™, 86
Board holism, 62
Board meetings. *See also* Planning
and effective decision making, 111–114, 169–171
idea-generating techniques in, 112–113, 173
importance of, 101–102
physical and procedural factors concerning, 107–110
principles of effective, 102–105
setting focused agendas for, 105–107

Board of directors. *See* Nonprofit boards
Board-regarding behaviors, 91
Boards, structuring of
advisory bodies and, 43–46
case study illustrating, 48–54
composition and diversity issues in, 39–43
criteria to evaluate, 35
examples of different, 35–36
foundations and, 46–47
size determinations in, 36–39
voting memberships and, 47–48
Boundary-spanning function, 139, 140
Boys and Girls Clubs, 99, 120
Boys Clubs, 120
Brain drain, 13
Brainstorming, 112–113, 173
Budgets, 6, 81
See also Finances
Buffer, 137
Bylaws, 20, 22

Carver, John, 5, 6, 93
Carver's model, 5–7, 61–62, 94
Center for Battered Women (CBW), 147
Chairperson, role of, 96–97, 111, 112
Charitable Gifts Fund, 86

Colorado Council of Boy Scouts, 36
Committees
  ad hoc, 57
  community and public relations,
    60–61
  executive, 58
  finance, 58–59
  fund-raising, 59
  nominating, 59–60
  program, 61
  resource development, 59
  role of, 56–57
  rules for effective, 62–63
  standing, 57
  structured under Carver's
    model, 61–62
  traditional, and their functions,
    58–61
  types of board, 57–58
Commonwealth Court (of
    Pennsylvania), 23
Conference Board, 69
Conflict, management of, 97–98
Consultant-expert model, 113
Corporate Council for the Arts
    (CCA), 121–123
Council on Foundations, 87
Craig Rehabilitation Hospital, 36
Cyclical board model, 7–10

Dayton Art Institute, 23
Decision Flow: Municipal League,
    105, 169–170
Decision making. *See* Board
  meetings
Decision tree, 107
Direct lobbying, defining, 25
Directors' and officers' (D&O)
    liability insurance, 22

Education
  benefits of board, 63–64
  new member orientation, 64–66
  systematic, 66–67
Empowerment, 89
Environmental scanning, 76–79
Equal Employment Opportunity
    Commission (EEOC), 25, 58
Errors and omissions insurance,
    22
Ethics. *See also* Accountability;
    Legal issues
  code of organizational, 30,
    159–160
  framework for an audit of, 31, 32
  and obligations of the board,
    28–32

Facilitator, 137
Fidelity Investment Company of
    Boston, 86
Fiduciary, defining, 17
Fiduciary obligations
  accountability and (*see*
    Accountability)
  ethical (*see* Ethics)
  legal (*see* Legal issues)
  Finances. *See also* Planning;
    Policies
  board's responsibilities
    concerning, 80–81
  budgeting, 81
  fund raising and (*see* Fund
    raising)
  key indicators of fiscal health, 82
Forward thinking, 120
Foundation boards, 46–47
Foundation for New Era
    Philanthropy, 149

Fund raising. *See also* Committees;
Finances
and changes in the resource
environment, 84–87
collaborative endeavors in, 142
legal issues and, 28
role of board in, 82–84

Gardner, John, 135
Girls Club of Denver, 12
Girls Incorporated, 98, 99
Governance. *See also* Fiduciary
obligations; Management
Carver's model of, 5–7, 61–62, 94
defining, 3–4
integrity of, 19
problems when boards prefer
management to, 11–14
tripartite system of, 4–5
Governance-theory model, 5–7,
61–62, 94
Government/nonprofit relations,
135–138
Grassroots lobbying, defining, 25
Group think, 39, 112

Haessly, Jacqueline, 104, 113
Heimovics, Richard, 91
Hereditary Disease Foundation, 121
Herman, Robert, 91
Hopkins, Bruce, 150
Hospice of the Florida Suncoast,
30, 48–54, 159–160
Houle, Cyril, 4

Immunity from civil liability
(Florida Statute), 157–158
Indemnification, defining, 22
Independent Sector, 37, 84, 135, 150

Institute of Policy Studies, 150
Institute of Public Service, 44, 45
Insurance, liability, 22
Integrity of governance, 19
Internal Revenue Code Section
501(c)(3), 20, 21, 26, 51
Internal Revenue Service (IRS)
Letter of Determination, 20–21

Job description, example of,
175–179
Job function, 93
John Ball Zoological Society, 104
John Hopkins University, 150
Joseph, James, 87
Judicial review, 101

Kiwanis, 141

Landers, Ann, 121
Leadership. *See also* Governance;
Management
contrasting, with management,
10–14
indicators to assess, 14–15
Leaky accountability, 18
Legal Action Center, 104
Legal issues. *See also*
Accountability; Ethics
board's responsibilities and
liabilities, 21–23
concerning board meetings, 101
documents basic to nonprofit
operation, 20–21
example of letter of agreement,
161–166
immunity from civil liability,
157–158
licensing requirements, 24–25

Legal issues *(continued)*
  regulatory issues and tax-
    exempt status, 23–24
  trouble spots and red flags,
    25–28
Letter of Agreement, 42–43,
  161–166
Letter of Determination, 20–21
Licensing, 24–25
Lobbying, 25–27
Louis Harris and Associates, 78

Management. *See also* Nonprofit
    boards
  of board/executive
    relationships, 89–95
  case study illustrating effective,
    98–100
  of conflict, 97–98
  of finances *(see* Finances)
  human resource, in boardrooms,
    95–98
  leadership versus *(see*
    Leadership)
  loss of perspective in *(see*
    Governance)
  overview of leadership and,
    10–15
  and performance assessment *(see*
    Performance evaluation)
  planning and *(see* Planning)
  policies of *(see* Policies)
  of relationships with
    government, 135–138
  and role of chairperson, 96–97
Materials, 6
Meetings. *See* Board meetings
Mergers, trend toward, 143–145
Milwaukee Peace Education
    Resource Center, 104

Mission
  benefits of focusing on the,
    120–121
  case study of challenges to an
    organization's, 121–123
  and importance of staying on
    track, 119–120
  and performance *(see*
    Performance evaluation)
  stating the, 117–119
Mission statement, 117–119
Model(s)
  consultant-expert, 113
  cyclical board, 7–10
  of governance *(see* Governance)
Municipal League of King County,
    105, 106
  decision flow of, 105, 169–170
  organizational cycle of, 105, 171

National Advisory Council of the
    University of Utah, 44
National Center for Nonprofit
    Boards (NCNB), 36, 40, 41, 57,
    61, 82
National Easter Seal Society, 138
National Mental Health
    Association, 48
Newman's Own™, 86
9–Box Tool, 77, 167–168
Nongovernmental organizations
    (NGOs), 126–127
Nonprofit boards
  background on existence of, 3
  categories of responsibilities for,
    55–56
  committees and *(see*
    Committees)
  core responsibilities of *(see*
    Finances; Planning; Policies)

development of (*see* Education)
and importance of mission (*see* Mission)
issues and challenges facing (*see* Nonprofit sector)
management and relationship issues for (*see* Management)
meetings and decision making for (*see* Board meetings)
models of (*see* Model(s))
obligations of (*see* Fiduciary obligations)
and principles of governance (*see* Governance)
structuring of (*see* Boards, structuring of)
Nonprofit sector. *See also* Nonprofit boards; Tax-exempt organizations
case study of adaptation in, 145–148
and changing role of executives, 139–140
collaboration and strategic alliances in, 140–143
government relations in, 135–138
image enhancement for organizations in, 148–150
impact of professionalism on, 138–139
and trend toward mergers, 143–145
Norms of reciprocity, 96
Northwest Network of Runaway and Youth Services, 139–140, 175

O'Connell, Brian, 37
On-site analysis, 79–80

Organizational Cycle: Municipal League, 105, 171
Orientation, new member, 64–66

Pathways for Women, 145–148
PAWS, 77
Perceptions, assessing, 167–168
Performance evaluation
board's role in, 123–125
executive, 127–129
list to aid boards in, 125–127
self-, by boards, 129–132
Permanent Endowment Fund (University of Utah), 44
Planned Parenthood, 142
Planning. *See also* Finances; Policies
for board meetings (*see* Board meetings)
board's role in, 75–76
environmental scanning in strategic, 76–79
long-range and strategic, 73–75
on-site analysis in strategic, 79–80
using 9-box tool in, 167–168
Policies. *See also* Finances; Management; Planning
categories of, 6–7
characteristics of, 69–70
developing fund-raising, 83–84
ends or executive limitations, 7, 94, 106
setting, 6, 71–73
six levels of, 70–71
Policy structure, 70
Political advocates, 137
Ponzi, Charles, 149
Position specification, example of, 175–179
Public Law 94–455, 26

Reciprocity, 96, 98–100
Regulations. *See* Legal issues
Resource dependency, 92
Robert's Rules of Order, 51, 110
Rules of conduct, 70

Salamon, Lester, 135, 150
Salvation Army, 29
Seattle-King County Bar
    Association, 21
Seattle University, 44, 45
Securities and Exchange
    Commission, 149
Shriners, 48, 77–78
Shriners Hospitals for Crippled
    Children, 48
Standard operating procedures,
    70
Standards of care, 21–22
SWOT (strengths, weaknesses,
    opportunities, and threats)
    analysis, 79

Tax-exempt organizations, 20
    See also Nonprofit sector
    benefits of, 21

regulations and (*see* Legal issues)
    types of, 155
Timed agenda, 105
Training. *See* Education
Tripartite system model, 4–5

Union Institute, 136
United Arts Fund, 121
United Way, 29, 42, 79, 90, 93, 130,
    145, 147, 149
University of Utah, 44
Unrelated business income, 27

Values guardian, 137
Voting memberships, 47–48

Washington Post, 149
Washington State Transportation
    Commission, 28
Wood, Miriam, 7, 10
Woodland Park Zoo, 119
World for Women, 145

YWCA, 147, 148

Zone of accommodation, 90